The Faith Factor
The Key to Black Empowerment

Keith Augustus Burton, Ph.D.

To Anne, Be empowered!

November 22, 2008

lifeHERITAGE Publications
Harvest, Alabama

THE FAITH FACTOR
Published by *life*HERITAGE Publications
P.O. Box 56, Harvest, AL 35749
www.lifeheritage.org

An earlier edition of this work was published under the title *We've Come This Far by Faith: and other spiritually awakening essays* (Huntsville, AL: A Voice in the Wilderness Publications, 1996).

All texts at the beginning of each chapter are from the *New Revised Standard Version*, Anglicized Edition (Oxford: Oxford University Press, 1998). All other translations and paraphrases were done by the author from the original languages.

Lyrics for the majority of the gospel songs, anthems, and spirituals are taken from J. Jefferson Cleveland and Verolga Nix, eds. *Songs of Zion* (Nashville: Abingdon Press, 1981).

Catalog Information

Library of Congress Control Number: 2004195252
International Standard Book Number: 0-9661803-2-1

Printed in Canada by Hignell Book Printing

10 09 08 07 06 05   7 6 5 4 3 2 1

τω διδασκαλω μου
και τω πατρι τω πνευματικω μου,
επισκοπω Ιακωβω Η Μελανσω,
πιστω διακονω

To my teacher and spiritual father,
Colonel James H. Melançon,
A faithful minister

Ms Rosa in Strength

The picture on the front cover is titled, "Ms. Rosa in Strength." It was created by Carlos Raphael of Louisville, Kentucky and is currently on display at the National Civil Rights Museum in Memphis, Tennessee. The collage depicts the painful struggle of the Civil Rights era with its interpretive portrayals of key figures. The stained glass frame reminds us of the crucial role of the Black church in the freedom movement. The intensity of the peaceful revolution is further represented by the fire hoses on the inner frame, the jagged canine teeth of police dogs, and the oversized tear drops reflecting a fragment of a "No Coloreds Allowed" sign.

TABLE OF CONTENTS

ACKNOWLEDGMENTS

People interested in securing this book will probably go to bookstores and libraries and request a copy of *The Faith Factor* by Keith Augustus Burton. However, no work is ever the product of one person's genius. If it were not for Neil Reid, who assigned me to deliver the keynote address for the 1987 Martin Luther King, Jr. Day chapel at Oakwood College, this book may never have been written. If it were not for Jeremiah Jasper who invited me to conduct a workshop on spirituality for the Black Methodists for Church Renewal in 1993, this book would never have been written. If it were not for Mervyn Warren for whom I became a "ram in the thicket" in 1995 when I responded to his sudden request to deliver a presentation on Black Moslems at the Annual Pastoral and Evangelism Conference, this book would never have been written. Had it not been for Leslie Pollard who solicited me to present workshops for the Oakwood College Men's Ministry department in 1996, this book would never have been written. Had it not been for Harold Cleveland who asked me to speak to the New Life Congregation about Christian Education, this book would never have been written.

This book is also the product of those willing soldiers who adjusted their busy schedules to read the manuscript in its rough stages and test the soundness of the message. These include Dr. Charles Bradford, a spiritual giant; Dr. James R. Doggette, an adventurous visionary; Dr. Pedrito Maynard-Reid, a model of *agape*; Dr. Philip Stubbs, a paradigm of determination; and Dr. David Williams, a prophet of justice.

The Faith Factor has also been blessed by the artistic

creativity of Mr. Carlos Raphael, who graciously granted permission for his award winning masterpiece to be used in the cover design. I would never have come in contact with Carlos had it not been for the unselfish concern of Ken Joslin, who has never met me but went out his way to find a fellow artist who could fulfill my stringent request. Dubbed "Ms. Rosa in Strength," the collage is currently on display at The National Civil Rights Museum in Memphis, Tennessee. I am deeply honored to have its imprint on this work.

As I extend kudos, how can I forget the masterful editorial finesse of Dr. Derek Bowe? His accurate eye and keen sense of aural aesthetics helped to smooth the flow of the language; while his sensitive heart challenged me to render a finished product that is less likely to offend certain segments of humanity. Thank you, Derek! This is a Christmas gift I will always remember.

Members of my immediate family have also made significant contributions to this book. My children, Sheereen and Kaleem, are constant reminders that the learned values that shaped my life are worth transmitting to successive generations. My wife, Hyacinth, serves as my subtle conscience in her constant encouragement for me to model what I preach. And, my parents, Nehemiah Augustus Burton and Cynthia Yvonne Morgan-Burton, continue to function as living chapters in the Divine edition of *The Faith Factor*.

There are countless other individuals whose example and encouragement have helped to prop up my faith in the midst of adversity. These have contributed to the "soul" of the book, and for that I am eternally thankful. Ultimately, the bulk of my appreciation is directed to the immortal YHWH, who is the ultimate object of our faith. May His name be praised for eternity. Amen.

Keith Augustus Burton
New Years Eve, 2004

INTRODUCTION

The *Faith Factor* is an enhanced revision of my earlier work *We've Come This Far by Faith* (1996). Written as a wake-up call to those in danger of falling into spiritual lethargy, this collection of essays has maintained its relevance as we confront the recurring challenges of living sanctified lives in a sin-drenched world. Like its predecessor, *The Faith Factor* will continue to encourage Christians to remain faithful to the God who has supported us through the turbulent past and sustains us in the tentative present.

Each chapter examines the role of faith in the spiritual experiences of Black people. Chapter one, "We've Come This Far by Faith," follows the transition of Black faith from its roots in Africa to the various contexts of Black American history. The second chapter, "It's Time," uses the monumental Million Man March to demonstrate how principles of faith preserved by the Nation of Islam have their roots in the Bible and are applicable to the Black Christian. In the third chapter, "An Affirmation of Black Manhood," Black men are encouraged to embrace the faith of our fathers and strive to be responsible husbands, fathers, spiritual leaders and mentors.

"Hakuna Matata," the theme of the fourth chapter, speaks to Black Youth and encourages them to be faithful to their divine call by developing a healthy self image, helping others and walking in the path of righteousness. Under the heading "Worldly Wine and a Perishing People," chapter five warns against the dangers that secularism and humanistic relativism pose to the Black community. In chapter six, a call is made for a united faith among African people as we undertake a critical exegesis of the civil rights theme "We Shall Overcome." The pace slows down in chapter seven, "One Village, One Child," as readers are encouraged to create an environment for children that will preserve, nurture and develop faith. Picking up speed, the final chapter, "The Walls Came Tumbling Down" contains a frank discussion on ecclesiastical racism as the faithful are summoned to launch an assault against divisive institutions.

A major addition to this edition is the list of study questions that follow each chapter. The study questions can be used for individual reflection or group discussion. If used for personal study, I suggest that you journal your thoughts and responses in a notebook. Group study can be conducted in a discussion format. Depending on the size of the group, the facilitator may wish to assign specific questions to smaller sub-groups who can discuss the issue and make a report to the larger group. Be sure to read the chapter *before* responding to the questions.

The eight-chapter structure of the book provides a rational for an eight-session study. However, feel free to adapt it to your individual needs. You may wish to cover a chapter a day during the seven days of Kwanza (with two chapters on the first or last day), or two chapters a day for weekly Bible study during Black History Month. You may even opt to devote more than eight sessions to the study of the book, and cover two or three significant questions at each group meeting.

The reader is strongly encouraged to utilize supplementary material while doing the exercises. A comprehensive Black History volume is a *sine qua non* for those who wish to dig beneath the surface. This will assist you in identifying names, events and places that I have not elaborated upon. For quick access to details in African-American history, I recommend John Hope Franklin, *From Slavery to Freedom. A History of Negro Americans* (8th ed. New York: Alfred A. Knopf, 2000).

As a result of engaging this book, the reader will develop the inner strength to counter the challenges of being Black in contemporary society. If the principles discussed in this book are put into practice, individuals and entire communities will be empowered to adapt a course of self-determination for their future.

While *The Faith Factor* addresses issues that affect the Black community, it also serves as a useful tool for our non-Black brethren who are seeking to gain a deeper understanding of our struggles, survival, and steadfastness. Since the book has been written from the painful experiences of one who lives with the reality of racism on a daily basis, some of the language may sound harsh to the non-Black reader. However, I have done my best to speak the truth in love, and I have no doubt that every open-minded reader will be spiritually rewarded. As you carefully select resources to help you navigate through the storms of life, I pray that *The Faith Factor* will earn its status as an indispensable addition to your Christian library.

CHAPTER ONE

"WE'VE COME THIS FAR BY FAITH"

Now faith is the assurance of things hoped for,
the conviction of things not seen. Indeed,
by faith our ancestors received approval.
(Hebrews 11:2)

No discussion about the African in the Americas can commence without examining the faith that has under-girded our existence. Indeed, it is faith as the "substance of things hoped for and the evidence of things unseen" that has allowed the nation, yea the world, to witness the stuff from which we are made. And that "stuff" is not our thick skin. It is not the psychological determination of M. Scott Peck's *The Road Less Travelled.*[1] It is not the psycho-neurology of L. Ron Hubbard's *Dianetics.*[2] But the stuff from which we are made is found in our resilient characters that have been fortified by the Spirit of the living God.

We have come this far by faith. Not faith in the government of the United States. Not faith in the White liberals who claim to be in our corner. But we have come this far by faith in the God who is able to move mountains if He so chooses—the same God who will sometimes allow the mountain to remain while fortifying us with the strength to climb.

Our faith experience has been the foundation of an exemplary spirituality that has garnered the attention of the world. While western and eastern European nations are joined by Asian communist powers that proclaim the death of God and the futility of religion, we have held on to our sure foundation. Sensing the void that results from a denial of the sacred in society, there has been a recent revival of spirituality in modern society. Self help gurus have proliferated and have produced countless books with detailed instructions about how people can reconnect with their spiritual selves.

Those seekers who purchased this book hoping to find the formula for faith or secure the secret of spirituality will have to look elsewhere. This is not going to be a "how to" discussion on spirituality. Spirituality is not a commodity that can be achieved by the mastering of a particular technique. You either have it, or you don't. In the New Testament book of Acts, Simon Magus approached the apostles and asked to buy the Spirit from them, but they had to send him away (Acts 8:9-20). The Spirit is not for sale. Spirituality is not something you put down in the week and pick up on church-days. It's who you are twenty-four hours a day, seven days a week, three-hundred-and-sixty-five days a year.

The concept of an ever-spiritual person is often hard to conceive in a society where there is a strong demarcation between the spiritual and the social—a society that is governed by the principle of hypocrisy. However, for the African there is no distinction between the sacred and the secular. There is no place in the African psyche for hypocrisy. Like Jesus of Nazareth when he spoke to the woman at the well in the Gospel of John, we believe that God is Spirit, and all those who worship Him must do so in Spirit and in Truth (Jn 4:24). Because God is Spirit, He is everywhere. And because God is Spirit, He is not limited to dark cathedrals with stained glass windows and lofty pipe organs. Because God is Spirit, He is everywhere I am, so I can praise Him anywhere, and I can live for Him every moment of my life. This knowledge of an all encompassing God is the essence of the spirituality of the African in the Americas and has its roots in the land of our fathers and mothers—**Africa.**

The African Legacy of Spirituality

Contrary to popular opinion, when the European slave traders invaded our idyllic paradise, we were not swinging from trees like monkeys and behaving like cannibals. We were not ignorant heathens who had no knowledge of God. We were a civilized people who were highly cultured and content with the life to which we had become accustomed. We had founded kingdoms from Timbuktu to the great architectural structures in the Kingdom of Venda in Old Zimbabwe. While many of us recognized the existence of numerous spirits, which some refer to as "lesser gods," the majority acknowledged that there was a unique God with whom the others could not compare. This Supreme being was responsible for the creation and maintenance of the universe, and we honored Him greatly with our lives. From our very inception, we were a spiritual people.

We brought our spirituality with us to the shores of the New World where it would eventually be re-contextualized within the framework of Christianity. We listened to the slave master talk about this Jesus who wanted us to remain servile and submissive, but he did not know that we already knew God for ourselves. As a result of our knowledge of God, rather than accept the heretical notion of a God who approved of slavery, our ancestors knew deep within their hearts that the Supreme God was a God who reacts favorably towards the faithful.

During this period, the recontextualization of our spiritual-ity was expressed in song through the Negro Spirituals. Some would like to relegate the importance of spirituals as they refer to them as American folk songs, or harp on the theory that they were used merely as codes for those wanting to escape to the illusionary paradise of the northern states. But in my heart of hearts, I know that the slaves believed what they sang. When things got too rough for them on the planta-tion, they would "steal away to Jesus" at the "hush harbor" meetings that often took place by the riverside. In these illegal gatherings, they would sing and pray in whispers—always prepared to muffle an ecstatic worshiper who became filled with the Spirit. After satisfying their spiritual thirst, they would leave the open air cathedral and return to their cabin cells, not knowing if the master would find out about their adventure and punish them for worshiping their sweet Jesus.

We held on to Jesus, for we knew He had been our help in ages past. He had been our help in the motherland when a drought threatened to damage our crops. He had been our help when our child was close to death with malaria. He had been our help when our spouse was considered infertile. We knew that our God was a mighty God. So in spite of our oppressed conditions, we remained faithful to Him. In spite of our constant desire for revenge, we maintained our spiritual-ity.

Our African legacy also aided us in allowing the Spirit to control our daily lives. Although most of us were illiterate during slavery, we had encompassed the golden rule, and God had written His law on our hearts. The ethics of our spirituality were expressed in Spirituals in such terms as: "Ain't gonna let nobody turn me round, keep on to Calvary. I would not be a liar, I'll tell you the reason why, for if my Lord should come and find me, I would not be ready to die." Fidelity to God was the driving force behind our existence, for we knew that there was a prize at the end of the struggle. And so although we were barefoot, bareback, and bareheaded, we could sing: "I've got shoes, you've got shoes, all God's chillun got shoes ...." One may call this quest for perfection works-righteousness, but our ancestors knew that faith without works is dead and that "Everybody talking 'bout heaven ain't going there." Only those who "Keep their hands on the plough and hold on" would see the kingdom of God.

Our spiritual grounding in the God of our ancestors is in marked contrast to the middle class European feminists who choose to humanize God by calling Him "mother" because of their negative experiences with males. I would like to remind the feminists that no group of women has been more negatively treated by males than our own mothers in slavery whose bodies were not theirs but masturbating tools for the slave masters and their sons.

Our mothers were victimized by these men, and their children were born as bastards in the sight of society, but their spirituality did not allow them to take it out on God and recreate Him in their own image. For indeed, it was sweet Jesus who had comforted them when massa was forcing his sex-craved torso on their ebony sweetened bodies. And when they and their children saw those unfeeling perpetrators who had fathered them going to their big houses with enough room to house an army while they had to huddle together in their one room cabin, they would sing, "Plenty good room, plenty good room, plenty good room in my Father's kingdom...." They had no place in the earthly house of their biological father, but their real Father would not cast them away. The God of their parents Abraham, Isaac, Jacob, Sarah, Rebecca and Leah, had plenty room for them in his estate (John 14:1-3).

Furthermore, our reference to God as "Father" in no way indicates an ignorance of a God who is all encompassing—a transcendent God who is beyond humanity. When the slave preacher sermonized, he remembered that someone from the motherland had made him know that the Arabic name for God is Allah—the all in all. Consequently, as he preached, he told those children who had just seen their mother sold off to another plantation, "If you're motherless, He'll be your Mother." He told that mother who had just lost her child after being forced to give birth in a freezing shack, "If you're childless, He'll be your Daughter." The God who is Allah—the all in all—was able to satisfy all the needs that our forbears could envision.

Spiritual Warfare after Emancipation

For many slaves, the victory of the Union soldiers in the Civil War marked the commencement of the "Year of Jubilee." But was this true? Had Abraham Lincoln been their Moses? Wasn't he the same man who said that if it were possible to save the union without freeing a single slave, then he would have done it?[3] Was this man their Moses?

The reality of the post-emancipation situation was that although "Jubilee" and "liberation" had been announced, there still was no cause to be *liberally jubilant*. The economy of the country in which they lived had depended for years on the slave population, and there was absolutely no way that this newfound liberty could be ushered in smoothly.

While many headed for the northern states, most faced the reality of their limited options and stayed on at their plantations as sharecroppers with a never-ending debt. And to make matters worse, the illusion of Reconstruction finally disintegrated when, three decades after emancipation, Plessy versus Ferguson was enforced by the federal courts. This ruling indicated the inception of legalized apartheid in the United States, a system that the Boer Afrikaners of Azania were to imitate in the early twentieth century.

This was *post-bellum* America, but only one war had been won—the war between the Unionists and the Confederates. The African people of America had to come to terms with the reality that another war was taking place—a *bellum spiriti*, a spiritual war. In truth, they were "not wrestling against flesh and blood, but against principalities, powers, rulers and spiritual wickedness in high places" (Eph 6:12). Nonetheless, in the midst of their condition, our people continued to prosper, for we knew "in whom we believed."

As we moved to the urban centers of America, we continued to sing, but our feelings were now expressed in the gospel song. Ours was the song of a liberating Jesus who had proleptically broken down the walls of partition that still separated us from our oppressors. But through it all, we sang:

Why should I be discouraged, Why should the shadows
    come,
Why should my heart be lonely, And long for heaven

and home,
When Jesus is my portion? My constant friend is He,
His eye is on the sparrow, And I know He watches me....
We knew that our hope was in the pilgrim who had gone on before and overcome the obstacles of bigotry, and so we sang:
Footprints of Jesus, leading the way
Footprints of Jesus, by night and by day
Sure if I follow, life will be sweet!
Saved by the prints of His wounded feet.

The American Nightmare

The reality of the spiritual war evoked several reactions from Black leaders. These leaders realized that the evil forces that controlled the minds of their oppressors were presenting an obstacle that prohibited our ancestors from realizing the American dream. *For the majority of us, the American dream was a living nightmare.*[4] We were those whom Paul describes as the children of the day surrounded by the predators of the night (1 Thess 5:1-11). We were pilgrims in a hostile environment as we waited for that "Great Day" to come that our parents sang about in the spirituals. And with the hope that had urged us on for three centuries, we continued to sing with implacable determination, "There's a sweet relief in knowing, the Lord will make a way somehow."

As we waited on the Lord, some in our midst believed that the Lord helps those who help themselves. One of the visionaries who broke from the mold was Booker T. Washington, founder of Tuskegee Industrial Institute. Washington believed that in order to find a meaningful place in this White world, the Negro needed to monopolize a certain market commodity. Then there was Dr. William E. B. Dubois who sought to appeal to the educated class in white America as well as encourage the development of a Negro intelligentsia—a "talented tenth" of Black educated professionals—who would help to elevate the masses. Later, Marcus Mosiah Garvey advanced the concept of "negritude" under the slogan "Africa for the Africans," with the dream of establishing a pan-African nation that would be a military and economic rival to the existing world powers.

In their push for the social and economic advancement of the race, each of these leaders was well aware that if we were to achieve success, we could not forget who had led us in the past. Among these pioneers, Garvey encapsulated this concept best with his creed:

Let no voice but your own speak to you from the depths. Let no influence but your own rouse you in time of peace and time of war. Hear all, but attend only to that which concerns you. Your allegiance shall be to your God, then to your family race and country.... Your Creed: "One God, One Aim, One Destiny."

Spirituality in Action

The practical spirituality promoted by Washington, Dubois and Garvey became the foundation of the Civil Rights Movement. Unlike the ethereal spirituality of reclusive mystics, African-American spirituality spoke to the body as well as the soul. It did not dwell in a constant state of denial, calling its adherents to meditate on a giant "pie in the sky." Instead, this tangible spirituality proposed that it was permitted for us to enjoy pie while living on this side of eternity. Faith did not demand its adherents to wait passively for a supernatural breakthrough, for "God helps those who help themselves." While this phrase is definitely not biblical, it does find affinity in James' declaration that "Faith without works is dead" (James 2:26). God is a helper, but He is not a waiter. If you are hungry and the Lord tells you there is bread around the corner, He expects you to go and get it. If you are disenfranchised and dispossessed and desire a voice in society, you must agitate the political status quo.

Our affinity to a practical spirituality was probably rooted in our African holism. We understood that our connection with divinity summoned us to greatness and not servitude. Initially bemused and befuddled by our abduction and resettlement in a strange land, we finally gathered the strength to stand up and be counted. We knew that God did not intend for us to be doormats for the oppressors' dirty boots. We had also learned something about our captor nation, and had determined that it was time for this country, which boasted of its Christian heritage, to understand the imperatives of the egalitarian gospel of Christ. This renewed vigor set the stage for the Civil Rights Movement.

There were two prongs to the fork of the Civil Rights Movement. The first belonged to the non-violent campaign spearheaded by Dr. Martin Luther King, Jr.'s Southern Christian Leadership Conference. Knowing that there was no way Blacks could influence the government through military or economic strength, King learned from Gandhi's struggles against the British crown and adopted the strategy of love.[5] King wisely noticed that love was the essence of spirituality. Indeed, doesn't Jesus identify the greatest commandment as "love to God" and "love to humanity"?

The Black church supplied the base for the segment of the Civil Rights Movement that was committed to non-violence. Many Black Christians firmly believed that their faith in the God who delivered the sons of Israel from Pharaoh in Egypt would not return void. They saw the struggle which lay ahead and looked back at the rugged path over which they had travailed, and with energized determination bellowed the anthem:

We've come this far by faith, Leaning on the Lord
Trusting in His Holy Word, He's never failed me yet
Oh, can't turn around, We've come this far by faith.

Although the fire hoses would be turned on them with a force so strong that it would lift them from the ground like fallen leaves floating in the wind, and although they were set upon by dogs, and beaten, lynched and imprisoned, their souls remained anchored in the Lord. They may have been outnumbered and overpowered by the forces of evil, but with the fuel of faith, they could prophesy:

We shall overcome, we shall overcome
We shall overcome some day,
Deep in our heart, we do believe,
We shall overcome some day.

Even when their leader's flesh was pierced by the assassin's bullet and yielded a spurt of blood which almost quenched their zeal, they were encouraged by Mahalia Jackson who echoed the immortal petition, penned by the recently-deceased Thomas Dorsey:

Precious Lord, take my hand,
Lead me on, let me stand
I am tired, I am weak, I am worn;
Thru the storm, thru the night,
Lead me on to the light,
Take my hand, precious Lord, Lead me home.

And the Lord continues to hold our hand, as in the absence of our Moses we are forced to remember in whom our strength really lies.

The second prong on the piercing fork of the Civil Rights Movement belonged to the Nation of Islam. Organized by former Baptist preacher Elijah Muhammad, and popularized by the son of a Garveyite Baptist preacher, Malcolm X (El-Hajj Malik el-Shabazz), the Nation of Islam was established on practical spirituality. Put off by the radical and confrontational rhetoric of Black Moslem leaders, many Christians have not learned to appreciate the central role of the Nation of Islam in the Civil Rights struggle. However, as Dr. James Cone recognized, the nonviolent movement would probably not have been successful if it were not for the militants who were willing to put their lives on the line in order to secure Black freedom. America was faced with two options, and it chose the one that seemed less threatening.[6]

Black Moslems taught that Civil Rights could only be attained when Blacks discarded European culture and institutions, creating a civil world for themselves. In this world, Blacks would run the schools, businesses and governments. They would even control the religious establishments, which would be free from the icons, menus and rituals that were used as tools to manipulate during the centuries of servitude. For the Black Moslem, spirituality is not an option but an integrated way of life.

Influenced by the philosophies of Marcus Garvey, the Black Moslems teach that in order for Blacks to attain any degree of economic success, they must first submit to Allah and order their lives accordingly. Their diet is reformed to ensure that Allah is served by the healthiest servants. Their dress is reformed so their minds can be kept pure and not made to wander into sexually perverted thoughts. Prayer is an intricate part of their lives, as they turn towards Mecca in meditation five times a day. Together with these spiritual exercises, the Black Moslem believes that the Black person must learn to do for him/herself and cannot depend on the White man. Tens of thousands of Blacks who were living the reality of the American nightmare have found this message attractive and have deepened their spiritual experiences by joining the Moslems. Although many have problems with their brand of theology, few would deny that the Nation of Islam still stands as a constant beacon of practical spirituality to this very day.

Conclusion: We've Come This Far by Faith
We now live in the post civil-rights era, and the symbols of our struggle are still visible. Members of the Nation of Islam continue to minister in the ghettoes and jails where they recruit and reform young African Americans who would otherwise end up in street gangs and ultimately the grave. We still see the central place that God holds in the Black community as we read the personal ads in *Ebony* in which singles request partners with strong spiritual values. Black educational institutions remain faithful to their religious heritages while their White counterparts are immersed in the sea of secularism. And although there are many amnesiacs who purport that God has let us down as a people, the majority of us still believe that God has kept us up, and indeed keeps on lifting us up until the day when we arrive at the place where we really belong.

Yes, my people, "We have come this far by faith!" And in celebration of our faithfulness, I submit that the record of those who have gone on before needs to be appended to the list of the faithful in Hebrews 11. If the Spirit would allow Sacred Writ to document our struggle, the record would contain the following:

By faith Nat Turner responded to the voice that compelled him to lead a rebellion against those who could "destroy his body but not his soul."

By faith Harriet Tubman repeatedly ventured into danger,

confident that the God who had secured her freedom could do so for countless others shackled in the bonds of slavery.

By faith Booker T. Washington founded Tuskegee Institute, knowing that since there was no room in "their" inn, we had to build our own.

By faith Marcus Mosiah Garvey founded the Universal Negro Improvement Association with the hope that Africans everywhere would unite and prove to the world who we really are.

By faith Rosa Parks refused to go to the back of the bus as she demonstrated that no race has the right to laud itself over another.

By faith Martin Luther King agitated the American conscience as he rallied the masses together to prove the true power of love over violence.

By faith Malcolm X complemented the Civil rights struggle as he stressed the necessity for Black people to defend their rights and improve their condition "by any means necessary!"

All these soldiers struggled in faith, not having received the promise but knowing in their heart of hearts that someday we will all be free.

Study Questions

1.   What is the central message of this chapter?

2.   Review the stories behind the characters featured in
      Hebrews 11:1-13, and provide a biblical definition of
      "faith."

[Note: The author of Hebrews uses terms from classical rhetoric to
define faith. He proposes that faith is a persuasive argument in favor
of the existence of God. In fact, the Greek word, *pistis*, is the technical
term for the argumentative sections of a speech that contain the
evidence for the thesis. The word for hope, *hupostasis*, refers to a
refutation argument that continues to poke holes in the argument of the
opponent. From a Christian perspective, the person of faith will never
allow our adversarial opponent to win his argument that God is not just.
By living a life of faith in the face of opposition, we provide evidence
for the existence and trustworthiness of God.]

3.   What is your reaction to the suggestion that economic,
      political, and social empowerment are expressions of a
      faith that works? Consider James 2:15-17 in your answer.

4.   Many people have suggested that slavery was God's way
      of introducing the gospel to Africans. Given our current
      awareness of the fact that the Axumite Ethiopian kingdom
      was among the first ancient nations to embrace Christian-
      ity, what is your response to this charge? Is slavery of God,
      or Satan?

5.   Recall the major events in the story of Job. Given the
      consistency of the African's faith in God during slavery, is
      it fair to compare the collective experience of Black
      people to the faith of Job? What hope can we glean from
      the story of Job?

6.   What is your reaction to the popular theory that the
      Negro Spirituals were merely codes that compared
      freedom in the northern states to eternal life in heaven?
      Did the slaves really believe in the coming kingdom of
      God?

7. Which one of the spirituals or gospel songs from the Black experience means the most to you? What are the predominant biblical themes in this song?

8. What other names could be added to the list of people of faith that concludes the chapter? Explain how each of the new names can be used as an example of faith.

9. Make a list of the five most important lessons you have learned from this chapter.

10. Reflect on how this chapter has affected you as a person.

11. Evaluate how this chapter has affected your relationship with God.

CHAPTER TWO

"IT'S TIME"
A CHRISTIAN RESPONSE TO
THE ISLAMIC CHALLENGE

For everything there is a season,
and a time for every matter under heaven.
(Ecclesiastes 3:1)

On October 16 1995, over one-million Black men from the contiguous states of the Union assembled at the nation's capital. This strong expression of unity was intended to show the world that the Black community is by no means a defeated foe. Black Christians have expressed two diametrically opposed reactions to the Million Man March on Washington. While the vast majority of those in attendance were Christian, an influential sector of the Black Christian community openly chastised those Christians who took part. The major problem for the opponents was the person in charge of rallying the masses together: Nation of Islam spiritual leader, the Honorable Minister Louis Farakhan. Somehow—maybe influenced by the rhetoric of Johnny Cochrane during the famous O. J. Simpson trial—they could not "separate the messenger from the message."

As I reflect on the vocality of some of the agitated Black leaders, I wonder if there is a subtle hypocrisy at play here. It is true that Louis Farakhan is not a model Christian—some may even question whether he is a model Moslem. Few Christians would accept the syncretistic compromising in his eloquent speech delivered on that memorable day. Few Christians would accept his myth about the rebellious Yakub who genetically engineered an inferior human species known as the White man. Few Christians would align themselves to his separationist attitudes brought on by the Nation's desire to establish a Black kingdom right here in the United States of America. Nonetheless, there is a subtle hypocrisy at play among those who oppose the Million Man March.

Even as some of our leaders have condemned Minister Farakhan for his divergent views, I am sure that not every Black Christian shares the secular humanism undergirding the New Age vision of Dr. Martin Luther King, Jr. However, when it comes to Dr. King, most of our leaders have been able to separate the personal theology of the messenger from his socially empowering message. Likewise, a significant number of those who provide us with religious music do not accord their lives in harmony with the word of God—with their creeping compromise and secret sodomizing—yet we continue to patronize them as we separate the messenger from the message and claim to receive blessings from their music.

I feel that it is imperative for us to look beyond the racist, misdirected and divisive rhetoric of the one in whose mind this statement of unity was planted while considering the stated intention of the march: a Day of Atonement for Black men. Didn't God use the Ethiopian prophet Balaam to speak to his people Israel? Didn't God reveal His will to the pagan procurator Pontius Pilate? In fact, judging from the massive response to the call by people who are not even affiliated with the Nation of Islam, this rally should probably have been summoned by a Christian leader. However, a stark reality is that while there are many Christian outreach projects in our inner cities, not enough Christian leaders have taken the initiative to do the kinds of economically and socially empowering things in the community that the Nation of Islam has been doing for decades. Consequently, the majority of Christian leaders do not have had the kind of rallying power that has been demonstrated by one representing a movement that has shown concern for Black men—misguided though some may perceive him to be.

Rather than cause further division in the community, I feel it necessary that Christian leaders look beyond the faults of the chief orchestrator and see the need of our people. Any honest person who is concerned with the plight of society will have to admit that the Black community is in disarray. As Black Christians, we need to be proactive in addressing the problems in the Black community since we can reach our people best. This does not mean that we are to neglect other ethnic groups, but our efforts are best channeled when directed towards those who can readily identify with us. And as the massive response to the Million Man March has made evident, "it's time."

Stop Blaming The Man for Our Problems

It's time, first of all, to stop blaming the White man for our current problems. We cannot overlook the fact that White Europeans have a history of oppressing the African. We were brought to the shores of the Americas as slaves and have never been fully accepted as citizens, since the system continues to find ways to exploit and exclude us.

Nonetheless, while some obstacles still remain, many have been eradicated. For instance, four decades ago a gathering of such magnitude in the nation's capital by Black men seeking unity and responsibility would have attracted the U.S. Army and probably legitimated an excuse for the government to inflict genocide. But on that balmy fall day in 1995, the constitutional right to assemble was exercised by our compatriots who have come to the realization that emancipation has taken place and we don't have to live with anybody's foot on our neck. Just by participating in the rally, the one-million plus Black men demonstrated that we are ultimately responsible for our own destiny.

Let us not think that the concept of self responsibility has its ultimate inception in the Nation of Islam. Long before the Nation permeated the inner city communities and encouraged Black men to give up crack and graduate from government handouts, the prophet Ezekiel opened our eyes to our responsibility to ourselves in the eighteenth chapter of his prophecies. He lets us know that despite the shortness of the end of the stick that we receive from the oppressor; in spite of the racist policies that exclude many of us from public life; in spite of the fact that jobs in our communities may be scarce and unemployment high, we cannot continue to blame our depraved condition and deficiencies on somebody else.

I cannot deny that slavery has been effective in demoralizing the Black man. I cannot refute the reality that slavery has been an instrumental part in the deterioration of the Black family structure. Our ancestors often grew up in single-parent homes; in fact, some even had to grow up in no parent homes. However, this was not by choice. Our mothers did not choose to be raped by the massa. Our fathers did not choose to live in a society where they could be sold to a new plantation at any time. We had no choice back then, but we do now.

Ezekiel says in no uncertain terms, "The soul that sins shall die" (Ezek 18:4). No White man forced any one of us to become stud machines and father children at such a rate that it is now estimated that almost seventy-five percent of Black babies are born into single-parent homes. We can't continue to blame The Man for our problems because contrary to a century ago, we now have choices, and "the soul that sins shall die."

We can choose to receive an education. We can choose where and who to marry. Obstacles have been lifted. While The Man may be putting drugs and alcohol in our communities, we are the ones who are buying and peddling them. While The Man may be producing the guns, we are the ones who are using them to kill each other. While The Man may be requiring a different quality of education for those in the "hood" and those in the "burbs," we are the ones who refuse to attend the school meetings where we can make a difference; we are the ones who refuse to support our own schools. While The Man may omit our faces from church literature and continue to propagate a myth of a biblical world that is void of Black people, we are the ones who refuse to pool our resources together and provide alternative literature that is racially inclusive. We can't continue to blame The Man for our problems, because we are responsible for our destinies.

Stop the Exploitation of the Black Community

Not only do we need to stop blaming The Man for our problems, but we also need to do something as Christians to stop the exploitation of the Black community. After the proclamation of emancipation, our ancestors were promised that the government would grant to them reparations for slavery amounting to forty acres of land and a mule. While this appeared to be a generous offering, there was fine print at the bottom of the contract that could only be read with an observatory telescope. What good is forty acres when we did not have the money to buy the ploughs, sickles, hoes, and the other agricultural equipment needed to run a successful farm? What did it mean to be a land owner if the *nouveau faux* gentry could not pay the government taxes? Furthermore, who was going to buy the crops once they were harvested? In a subtle way, the system ensured that the Black man would always be dependent on the oppressor for his necessities.

The success of this dependency program is portrayed in the reality that while Blacks in the United States have a combined earning that surpasses the GNP of Canada, less than fifteen-percent of our money is used to patronize Black business. Somehow we have been programmed to think that if one of our own is the boss, we ought to get the goods for free; and when that person lays down sound business principles, and refuses to let us suck them dry, we defiantly take our money across the street to the store that didn't even allow us to use their bathrooms thirty years ago.

The Million Man March aimed to demonstrate the economic potential of the African in America. We don't need to spend our dollars in businesses that are run by people who don't want us living in their neighborhoods. We don't need to fatten the pocket of those who are fighting Affirmative Action because they don't want us to work for their companies. We don't need to grease the palms of those who would rather hire illegal aliens for a pittance than pay some of us a minimum wage so that we could be released from the chains of government dependence.

Under Elijah Muhammad, the Nation of Islam proved to the world that the so-called Negro in America did not have to remain victim to the exploitation of the oppressor. The Nation purchased land in rural America and operated farms which supplied fresh produce to Black owned markets in urban America. It also established banks, schools, restaurants, and other businesses that served Chicago's South Side, employing many who were not even members of the Nation.

But here again, let's not think that the concept of resisting exploitation is something that the Nation of Islam invented, for the word of God lets us know in Micah 6:8 that the LORD requires all of us to "to do justly, and to love mercy, and to walk humbly with our God." And again through Amos He proclaims, "Let justice roll down like waters, and righteousness like an everlasting stream" (5:24). Those who claim to be the people of God ought to be doing something about injustice, and the greatest injustice against our people is the systematic exploitation of our communities.

While we do not and cannot promote separate states as the Nation of Islam does, we realize that we have an economic potential that could liberate us financially. There is no reason why over eighty-five per-cent of Black dollars in this country is used to support White businesses. There is no reason why most church members should be living in rented accommodations in urban America, and paying money to a faceless slum-lord in the suburbs, when, if they pooled their resources, they could build or buy their own apartment complexes. There is no reason why our larger churches should be plagued with unemployment, when the physical, intellectual, and financial resources are available to initiate restaurants, supermarkets, clothing factories, nursing homes, child-care centers, tutoring programs, credit unions, consulting agencies, and construction companies. It's time to stop the exploitation in our communities, and *you* are the vehicle for averting the onslaught.

Recover Our Spiritual Roots

Not only is it time to stop blaming the man for our problems and to put an end to the exploitation of the Black community, but it is also time to recover our spiritual roots. When the White man abducted us from our homeland, we were not swinging from trees and eating each other. We were not heathen infidels who were ignorant of the immortal, invisible, God who created the heavens and the earth. We were a spiritual people who fashioned our lives after the mandates of the Almighty. In fact, it is not until the western missionaries and their accompanying colonizers invaded the continent that the concept of atheism was introduced to our people. In spite of where one lived on the fabricated continent of Africa, the existence of God was a *sine qua non*.

The Million Man March was successful in illuminating the spiritual roots of Black people. While we may not agree that our spiritual roots are to be found in the religion of the Arabs that was imposed on some Africans in very much the same way as Christianity was, all observant people are forced to agree that the problems in our communities can only be solved by the Spirit of God.

Our Moslem brethren may have a genuine concern and noble motives, but they don't have the facts together. We need to let them know that the original religion of the African is not Islam. We need to let them know that the Supreme God is known by many names, only one of which is Allah. We need to let them know that long before the colonizing Arabs spread their influence in Ghana and Nigeria, our people were worshiping *Chi-Neke*—the Ebo appellation for the God of creation; our people were worshipping *Onyame-kwame*—the Akan designation for the God whose day is Sabbath.

They need to know that for many millennia, African people were not attending mosques on Fridays or Cathedrals on

Sundays, but every Sabbath, communities around the continent assembled to worship the Almighty God—the Lemba and Vamwenyi of Southern Africa; the Meru, Kalinjeni, and Luo of East Africa; and the Akan and Ebo of West Africa. They also need to know that Africa embraced Christianity before any European nation, and before Islam even existed. And even to this day the Ethiopian Orthodox and Egyptian Coptic Churches betray their biblical roots in their recognition that the day of celebration to the Creator is God's holy Sabbath.[1]

Conclusion: The Messenger and the Message

In conclusion, I would like to reiterate my contention that there are times when it is necessary to separate the messenger from the message. We cannot refuse to take seriously the problems in our communities for fear that people may mistake us for Moslems. No religion has the monopoly on compassion and community empowerment. Christians have become so intentional about being "different" that many in the community view Christianity as irrelevant. However, the gospel of Christ demands that we take the lead in promoting the principles underlying the Million Man March and the social tenets undergirding much of the Nation of Islam's activity.

I am well aware that the major doctrines of the Nation of Islam are incompatible with Christianity. I don't have to be told that the nation is a counter cultural religion that is centered around the syncretistic, esoteric, and racialist teachings of Elijah Muhammad and Louis Farakhan. I don't have to be told that the ultra-fanciful Myth of Yakub and the account of the origin of the human race is informed by evolutionary theories and is contrary to the Bible and the Koran. I don't have to be told that the request for separate states for Black people in the USA does not match up to the biblical vision of the New Heavens and New Earth which will be inhabited by people from all nations, kindred, tongues and people. I don't have to be told that Wallace Fahd Muhammad is neither the returned Christ nor Allah in the flesh, for the Bible attests that "there is only One God and one mediator between God and humanity" (1 Tim 2:5).

Nonetheless, I believe that somehow the Million Man March

has been used as an instrument by God to let us know that it's time to do what we are supposed to be doing on the eve of His return. I say again that I know that some may object to the messenger who was chiefly responsible for calling the march, but didn't Balaam speak for God? Didn't God use nations other than Israel as instruments for His Divine cause? Notice that God's use of those outside His chosen camp in no way made them holy, but God used them anyhow. Our response should not be to chastise the Nation of Islam because its teachings are incompatible with Christianity—it does not claim to be Christian. Instead, we need to capitalize on this opportunity to do the practical work of the gospel as we proclaim the reality that it is not Wallace Fahd Muhammad, it is not Elijah Muhammad, it is not Louis Farakhan Muhammad, but it is Jesus who saves. Fellow Christians, "It's time!"

Study Questions

1. What is the central message of this chapter?

2. Carefully analyze Ecclesiastes 3:1-8. Can these verses be used to support the argument that God-fearing Blacks should be involved in issues that affect the Black community?

3. What was your initial response to the Million Man March? Why do you think Black leaders had different opinions about the march?

4. Do you agree with the author's premise that God can use any vehicle to fulfill His will? (Consider the story of Balaam in Numbers 22-24.)

5. How much responsibility should the European-influenced West accept for the current social ailments that affect Black people?

[There is no doubt that institutionalized racism has negatively affected Black people around the globe. Slavery thrived on the destruction of the Black family. Not only were Blacks abducted from their African homelands, but when they were brought to the Americas, they were prohibited from creating solid family structures. Black families could be separated for economic reasons. Black men were encouraged to be stud machines with no responsibility to the children they fathered. Further, Black children had no professional role models to which they could aspire.]

6. How does Ezekiel 18:1-4 speak to the claim that the new freedom afforded to Blacks empowers them to rectify some of the social ailments in the Black community?

7. How can Acts 2:44-47 and Acts 4:32-35 help the Black Christian in the quest for economic independence?

[It is fallacious to assume that *all* Black people will cooperate in the quest for economic empowerment. There is too much mistrust between us–a mistrust that predates slavery, but that was definitely intensified by it. However, the nation of Islam has demonstrated that any community with a common identity can experience economic success. In fact, many Christian communities have managed to break the chains of economic slavery. As early as the 1920's, a Seventh-day Adventist minister, James K. Humphrey launched economic ventures in Harlem, New York. One of the more recent successful models is that of U.S. Congressman, the Reverend Floyd Flake, whose AME church in Jamaica, New York, has become a thriving multi-million dollar corporation, employing hundreds of people. I propose that every Black church community should be an economic zone.]

8.   How does the recovery of spiritual roots help to affirm identity?

9.   What expressions of Eurocentric religion have affected Blacks the most?

[Naim Akbar calls our attention to the negative effect that European religious art has had on the self image of Black people.[2] European religious influence has also caused some Black people to shun the expressive traditions in worship, which are an intricate part of African religion. Probably the biggest influence that Europe has had on Africa is the introduction of *Sunday* worship. The Ethiopian Orthodox and Egyptian Coptic churches honored the Sabbath for centuries before the Jesuits infiltrated their churches. Further, even the non-Christian Ghanaian Akan worshipped Onyame Kwame, the God whose day is Saturday.[3] In fact, the Akan refereed to the European missionary as Brunei Kwesi, "white man who brought Sunday." Millions of independent African Christians on the continent have rejected the imperial Sunday for the liberating biblical Sabbath.]

10. Make a list of the five most important lessons you have learned from this chapter.

11. Reflect on how this chapter has affected you as a person.

12. Evaluate how this chapter has affected your relationship with God.

CHAPTER THREE

AN AFFIRMATION
OF BLACK MANHOOD

*Then the LORD God formed the man from the dust of the
ground, and breathed into his nostrils the breath of life; and
the man became a living being.*
(Genesis 2:7)

As I encounter the multitude of menalin enriched faces that
bring contrast and variety to this society, I am forced to
admit that our survival is nothing short of a miracle. Any
logical prognosis of the atrocities we have suffered as a
people would have to conclude that we should not be

here—we should be extinct. As I contemplate the reality of the racially divided society in which we live and in which racist bigots are still burning churches, I cannot help but feel that we should not be here. As I cast my mind to a century ago when it was illegal in some states for Blacks to receive an education, I cannot help but feel that we should not be here. As I reel in shock at the citizens of Alabama, who voted in the 2004 elections to keep segregation era language in the State constitution, I cannot help but feel that we should not be here. But we *do* exist, and our existence is a living witness that there is a God who hears and answers prayers. We are a witness to the world that the Spirit of God is able to transform minds more oppressive than Pharaoh's. For this very reason, I find it necessary to affirm Black manhood in this chapter.

I understand that some may be wondering why we need to affirm Black manhood. Unfortunately, many of us suffer from CTS (Clarence Thomas Syndrome) and feel that we need to stop harping on the injustices that have been continually meted out to us. But how can we forget? How can we forget when we have elected politicians who contribute inflammatory rhetoric to the flames of white hatred that still blaze in this country? I say again that we need to celebrate Black manhood because in the wake of the Tuskegee Syphilis experiment[1] and the racial theories behind the AIDS epidemic,[2] it's a miracle of God that we have survived. This is not the time to debate the propriety of showering kudos on the African male—let's affirm Black manhood!

Others may be asking, "What about Black womanhood?" This is a fair question, but one has to admit that many of the problems in our community are caused by the deficiencies of the Black male. This is a legitimate concern for the Black community, and we can't allow ourselves to be influenced by those white liberals who oppose the principles behind male establishments like the Citadel—there is a time and place for men to be with men. We've seen the *queer* results of trying to play down the differences between the sexes.

The truth is that while we love our women, we have to recognize that men and women have different experiences. While some men would like to think they are women, they will never know how it is really like to be a woman. They don't have to experience a menstrual cycle and its monthly inconveniences. They will never know what morning sickness is all about. They will never experience menopause. That is why there is a need to affirm Black manhood, so we can address those issues that affect the Black man—and ultimately the Black society. Now that we have hopefully alleviated the objections, a single question remains: "How do we affirm Black manhood?" I will answer this question in four parts.

Manhood and Blackness

First of all, in order to affirm Black manhood, we have to understand the relationship between manhood and blackness. What does it mean to be a "Black man?" I have to make it clear that being Black has nothing to do with the color of your skin. If the truth were told, there are very few people in the world whose skin can really be defined with the adjective "black." In our communities, we are faced with a complexity of shades that betray our complex history. No, "Black" is not a descriptive adjective but a proper noun that describes an experience.

The experience associated with blackness is characterized by hardship and toil. An experience of abduction, subjugation, servitude, humiliation and segregation. A real Black man is one who can identify with his ancestors and compatriots in apartheid nations, although he may not have experienced oppression at the same magnitude as they. But not only does blackness symbolize hardship and toil, but it also stands for resilience and survival—like the Dutch Pot or Wok that becomes tougher with age. It conjures the spirit of the great poet of the Harlem Renaissance, the Jamaican-born Claude McKay, who wrote in the midst of adversity:

If we must die, let it not be like hogs
Hunted and penned in some inglorious mob
While round us bark the mad and hungry dogs
Making their mock at our accursed lot.

Being Black is about dignity—it's about having the dignity to stand tall when somebody calls you a "boy." It's about remembering how your male ancestors had to bite their lips and suppress their warrior mentalities while the slave master raped their wives and sold their children to other plantations. And let's remember that they did not do this because they were weak or afraid, but these strong men knew that in spite of their depraved conditions, they still had a responsibility to their families. Yes, among all races of men who have lived in recent history, none has more to affirm than the Black man who has been cast in the fiery furnace and has emerged with renewed strength to fight another day.

Manhood and Womanhood

Secondly, the process of affirming Black manhood involves the relationship of manhood to womanhood. One thing I have to make clear is that in the same way that Blackness is not defined by the color of one's skin, manhood is not defined by the possession of a certain anatomical appendage. Following in the legacy of our former owners, many Negro males feel that their manhood is proved by how many children they father. This attitude is no different from the slave masters and their adolescent sons who used our foremothers as masturbating tools.

Too many of our young men view fathering a child as a "rite of passage" into manhood. I would like to let my young brothers know that there is nothing uniquely manly about making babies. Any fool can father offspring. Those of us who call ourselves men need to start taking responsibility for our actions. For too long it has been the onus of the woman to say "no." Men have deceived themselves into thinking that she is playing "hard to get." However, a real man will be able to exercise the kind of self-restraint it takes to allow our women to remain ladies. A real man will be controlled and disciplined enough to let his date know that he is willing to wait until marriage before undertaking the serious responsibility of fathering children.

I would also like to say that Black manhood is not affirmed by the subjugation of Black women. Many of our men have the oppressor mentality. They feel that their self worth is dependent on making someone else feel inferior. They are not happy unless their foot is on someone's neck. And the most vulnerable victims for these cowardly excuses for men are our own Black women. These men are too weak to go out into the arena of life and confront the oppressor, so they turn on their own women. They disrespect their women so much that some see nothing wrong in referring to their sisters and mothers as female dogs and prostitutes. This atrocity is an outgrowth of the abuse that women have suffered in our communities for centuries, and should no longer be tolerated.

What Black men need to realize is that when God created man, in a very real way woman was a part of him. Indeed, her rib was fused among his, and when God had shaped the voluptuous ebony-sweetened Eve, Adam could truly say, "This is bone of my bone, and flesh of my flesh" (Gen 2:23). Our women are a part of us, and we need to respect them as much as we respect ourselves. In fact, according to Paul in Ephesians, no real man will abuse his wife, either verbally or physically, for in so doing he is abusing his own body (Eph 5:28-29). A real man is willing and ready to treat his woman like a queen. Yes, in order to affirm Black manhood, the Black man must recognize his responsibility to the Black woman.

Manhood and the Family

Thirdly, not only does an affirmation of Black manhood consider the implications of one's blackness and how the Black man ought to relate to the Black woman, but it also evaluates the place of manhood in the family. Despite the claims made by the radical arm of the feminist movement which desires to turn all women into male clones, God still has an ideal place for men and women in society. These God-ordained roles have nothing to do with the equal worth that is inherent in both man and woman, but they have been predetermined for the sake of preserving order in the community. While the face of society is changing, the immutable word of God lets us know that God in his wisdom has determined that the man should be the spiritual leader and backbone of his home.

I dare say today that one of the major causes for the breakdown of order and respect in the Black community is the absence of a positive male figure in the home. Before I continue, I would like to commend those single mothers who have been the strength and backbone of our communities. I would also like to commend the products of single-parent homes who—in spite of negative circumstances—have been able to stay focused and are determined not to duplicate the mistakes of the past. However, no matter how good a mother is, and how well she can fill that void, she can never be a father.

What we need today are Black Men who are sensitive enough to live up to their responsibilities. We need Black Men who realize that their sixty seconds of uncontrolled ecstasy can result in a lifetime of disaster for that woman who may have to relinquish her future aspirations as he moves on to the next one night stand. And lets not forget those children who may be forced to live a life of poverty and depravation. Black men, if you are not ready to say "I do" before the preacher, at least have the self restraint to say "I won't" when it comes to premarital sex. If you are not ready to take on the obligations of a family, then at least have the dignity to act responsibly.

And those of us Black men who are fathers and husbands need to realize that these appellations are not just titles, but they are an indication of our roles. There are many homes that might as well be single-parent because the father is hardly ever there, and when he is, he has no time for the family. I do recognize that society has placed an immense economic chain around our necks, but we cannot let our desire for material goods take us away from our families. As Black men we need to be towers of strength in our families as we learn the positions of priest and leader. Only when we are focused on our families will we truly be in a position to celebrate Black manhood.

Manhood and God

Finally, and most importantly, an affirmation of Black manhood is not complete until our manhood is placed in divine perspective. When affirming our blackness, there is always a danger of falling into idolatry. We can get so caught up in our being "Black" that "Black" soon becomes an object of worship. But we need to remember that we are only Black because God has fortified us with His grace. Let's not forget that we only survived the atrocities of slavery and segregation because we have a heavenly Father who watches over us.

In our affirmation of Black manhood, while we remember Carver, Malcolm, Martin, L'Ouverture, Cudjoe, Spinoza, Augustine, Solomon, Selassie, Marley, Evers, Turner, Walker, Foy, Cleveland, Bradford, Mandella, Kisseka and Garvey, let us not forget that these men were responding to a higher power. They were responding to the command of the God of heavens who desires liberty and justice for all people. And the same God that worked through these men in their efforts to liberate people shackled in the bonds of oppression is the God who lets us know in Galatians 3:28 that our Black Manhood means nothing if we are not fully surrendered to Him.

In seeking a connection with God, let's not get caught up with these reactionary movements that promote a God who only favors a certain race. The God whom I serve is not a territorial God. He is not a God who only functions on my terms. He's bigger than that. He is the God of the entire universe. He is the God who can save whom he desires, and it's none of my business whether that person is Black, White, or indifferent. He is the God who revealed himself to Moses with the words, *iyeh aser iyeh*—"I am what I am," and "I shall be what I shall be!" My God is not Black, my God is not White, my God is not Middle Eastern—in fact the only adjective I can use to describe God is God! God is God! And it is only because God is God that I can affirm my existence as a Black man who has been saved and sanctified. Yes, the God of the heavens and earth has given me a reason to affirm Black manhood.

Conclusion

In conclusion, as we bring our affirmation of Black manhood to a close, let us be aware of what we are really affirming. We are not involved in a separatist crusade like the Nation of Islam and other Black nationalist movements. We believe that we can affirm both the unity that comes from being *in* Christ and the diversity that characterizes our historical and cultural experience. In affirming Black manhood, we celebrate the history that has made us Black when we passed through the refining fire and claimed our place among the 144,000 seen by the Prophet John in Revelation (Rev 7:1-8; 14:1-5). In affirming Black manhood, we applaud our women who have constantly remained strong through these years of toil, and who deserve our greatest honor and respect. In affirming Black manhood, we support our families which provide us with encouragement and hope for a brighter tomorrow. And finally, in affirming Black manhood, we honor our God who is able to do exceedingly abundantly above all that we can ever think of asking. I invite you to join me in this affirmation of Black manhood.

Study Questions

1.   What is the central message of this chapter?

2.   What is your understanding of the statement that the first humans were created in the "image of God"? In other words, how do Genesis 1:26-28 and 2:7 impact your self image?

[The Nations of Gods and Earths (aka "The Five Percenters"), as well as some Rastafarian groups reason that since humans were first created in the image of God, then the Black man *is* God. However, remember that while originally created in God's image, Adam and Eve's decision to succumb to temptation resulted in the loss of that image. However, the sacrifice of Christ on Calvary has made it possible for all who are faithful to God to reclaim their original image through faith (see 1 Jn 3:1-3).]

3.   What does it mean to be a Black man in today's society?

4.   Discuss the author's contention that blackness is not determined by the color of one's skin.

5.   How does Ephesians 5:25-33 address the relationship between a *real* Black man and his wife?

6.   We know that the racist system has been responsible for destroying the Black family. However, the Black male is to be held responsible for contributing to the current state of the Black family. Too many Black men are responsible for fathering many and parenting none. The resultant single parent homes have affected the image of young Black males who continue to perpetuate the cycle. What can *you* do to lessen the negative impact of single parent families in the Black community?

7.   What is the significance of the contribution of Black

women to the survival of the Black community? Is it true to say that Black women have been the "backbone" of the Black community? Analyze the image of the virtuous woman in Proverbs 31:10-31, and discuss how it relates to the role of the Black woman?

8. What are the inherent dangers of indulging an afrocentricity that claims goodness and divine graces for the Black nation and demonizes the Europeans? In other words, does one have to hate White people in order to promote Black pride?

[One of the greatest dangers lies in the reality that there are more than two ethnic groups in this world. Where does the Asian or Hispanic fit in the Black/White schema?]

9. Make a list of the five most important lessons you have learned from this chapter.

10. Reflect on how this chapter has affected you as a person.

11. Evaluate how this chapter has affected your relationship with God.

CHAPTER FOUR

"HAKUNA MATATA"

If the dead are not raised,
'Let us eat and drink, for tomorrow we die.'
(1 Corinthians 15:32)

The "Lion King,"[1] a classic Disney animation, follows the story of Simba, a young lion cub who is heir apparent to the throne. Following his father's death, which was orchestrated by his wicked uncle Scar, Simba is pursued by conniving hyenas who leave him for dead in the vast African desert. Fortunately, Simba is rescued by Timon, an excitable muskrat, and Pumba, a portly warthog. This odd couple selfishly adopts Simba into their circle for the future benefits that would be theirs from having a lion as a friend. They are quick to acquaint Simba with the philosophy with which they conduct their lives. This philosophy is summed up with the Swahili (and Motswana) phrase, "Hakuna Matata" (a synonym to the

Jamaican unofficial motto, "No problem!") which they loosely
translate, "no worries for the rest of our days." This was their
problem-free philosophy—Hakuna Matata.

Simba adopted this philosophy and lived a life of
pleasure—eating, drinking and having fun. One day, Simba
rescued his friend Pumba from a lioness who was about to
devour the terrified warthog for dinner. During the confronta-
tion between the two ferocious felines, Simba discovered that
the one who was about to eat his friend was Nala, a lioness
who had been betrothed to him in her infancy. As the two
friends got reacquainted, Nala reminded him that while he
was living a carefree life with his uncommitted friends, there
were greater responsibilities waiting for him. In a harsh but
gentle way, she let her friend know that the Hakuna Matata
Philosophy he had adopted had forced him to forget from
whence he had come.

The Apostle Paul was also aware of the dangers that come
with a Hakuna Matata mentality. In his first letter to the
Christians in Corinth, Paul informs his audience that since Christ
has been raised from the dead, all those who profess to be his
followers have no business living their lives to the tune of
Hakuna Matata. He cajoles that if Christ has not been raised
from the dead, and if there is no hope for us, then "let us eat,
drink, and be merry, for tomorrow we die" (1 Cor 15:32). In
no uncertain terms, Paul is saying that the version of the
Hakuna Matata Philosophy promoted in the "Lion King" is only
for those who do not wish to participate in the kingdom of
God.

As I reflect on this text, I have to come to terms with the
sad reality that many professed Christians have adopted the
Simba mentality and have chosen to conduct their lives as if
they have no responsibilities. If the truth were told, at some
time in our Christian experience we have all acted as if Christ
has not been raised from the dead. All of us have experienced the magnetic pull of the worldly forces that mitigate
against our desire to embrace the Divine mandate. This is
especially true for our youth who are bombarded with so
many choices in their formative years that it often seems
easier to take the path of compromise and postmodern

apathy. In this chapter, I will draw three lessons from the "Lion King" that serve as a warning to those who have embraced the Hakuna Matata philosophy as a template for their lives.

Self Accountability

In my analysis of the movie, it soon became clear that the Hakuna Matata philosophy has devastating effects on one's self accountability. According to the laws of hereditary, after the death of his father Simba was the king. He was the one who was destined to rule the vast Prideland. The mere fact that he was alive made his kingly status a reality. Yet, he felt content to live a life of fun and spontaneity with the dubious duo, Timon and Pumba.

While the Lion King is a fictitious portrayal of animal life, a real analogy can be drawn between Simba and the countless people who have consciously shaken their true identity. In the beginning, God created men and women in His image. We are all His sons and daughters. However, many to whom God has been revealed have rejected their status as sons and daughters of the Most High, instead finding their identities in popular culture and secular society.

We also see this irresponsible attitude being acted out on a daily basis within our very midst. Many of our young people have no sense of accountability. They have bought into the negative media image of themselves. They believe the lies that are being propagated in racist literature like the *Bell Curve*.[2] They have become accustomed to simply "getting by." They opt for the easier path because they don't want to put in the time and effort it takes to achieve in life. They have no problem spending hours a day playing with video games and gossiping in Internet chat-rooms, but find it an inconvenient task to spend five minutes in the library. One who adapts a "no worry, problem free" philosophy often lives his or her life with the sole purpose of achieving pleasure. If it feels good, do it! Don't worry about the consequences.

When an individual chooses to conduct his or her life with a Hakuna Matata philosophy, a modified version of Sir Isaac Newton's third law of motion is always operative: "For every action, there is a reaction." It may not always be equal and opposite, but be assured, there will be a reaction. A few seconds with a needle in your arm or a joint in your mouth may end up in a lifetime of homelessness and mental illness. Thirty seconds of premarital sex—protected or unprotected—may end up in an unwanted pregnancy, a single-parent home, AIDS, or a lack of commitment to the one to whom you eventually get married. An attitude of "C-ing" your way through school, rather than putting in the extra effort it takes to make "As" and "Bs," may result in a lifetime of regret as society views you as mediocre, and you prove right the opponents of Affirmative Action.

In spite of the obstacles that face our youth, those who have a sense of pride and self accountability will rise to the occasion. If you don't believe me, ask Sister Maya Angelou, who from the ages of seven to twelve was diagnosed as a voluntary mute and never uttered a word during those five years.[3] Yet deep within her soul, she knew that one day she would talk again. With obstinate determination, she blocked out the chants of the taunters who labeled her dumb and tuned in to her grandmother who gave words of encouragement while she combed her wooly hair. And now Sister Angelou is a distinguished professor of Latin, French, and Literature, at Wake Forest University. She is also a poet laureate and an international celebrity.

Like Sister Angelou, you too can rise. But in order to rise, you have to shake of those negative stereotypes that have been planted in your mind by a racist and oppressive system. In order to rise, you have to discard those gangsta rap and dancehall CDs and DVDs that promote illicit sex and violence and refer to your mothers and sisters with epithets that describe female dogs. In order to rise, you have to start taking life seriously and stop hoping that the government will provide all of your wants and needs. Yes, in order to rise, you must reject the Hakuna Matata Philosophy that affects self-accountability.

Accountability to Others

A second consequence of the Hakuna Matata Philosophy is the effect it has on a person's sense of accountability to others. While Simba was enjoying a carefree life with his friends, his kingdom, the Prideland, was in ruins, and the people were miserable and oppressed. When Nala urged him to return and make an attempt to make things better, Simba shirked his responsibility and even had the audacity to invite her to join him in his complacency.

Here again we see an analogy of a picture that occurs too often in our midst. Unlike the first group whose adoption of the Hakuna Matata philosophy leads them to disrespect their own bodies, this second set is so occupied with self that the needs of others are neglected. These are the people who are too self-righteous or just plain afraid to get involved. These are the people who see an abusive man taking advantage of God's daughter whom he presumes to view as "his" woman, and reason that they do not have a right to intervene. These are the people who view education as a passport out of the ghetto and not as a tool to elevate the teaming masses of our people who have been taught by a racist system that ignorance is bliss.

Once a year, the Nation pauses to remember the birth and life of Dr. Martin Luther King, Jr. Compared to other Negro children of the Jim Crow era, King was born with a silver-plated spoon in his mouth. His middle class family possessed the pecuniary means to send him to the best schools and universities. As a result of his privileged status, combined with his natural talents, by the age of twenty-five, Martin Luther King was awarded a Doctor of Philosophy in Systematic Theology from the esteemed Boston University.

Like many Blacks who had made similar achievements in his day, King could have easily joined the faculty of a prestigious school and adopted the Hakuna Matata Philosophy of so many Blacks who have made strides in this White world. But, no! King chose the road less traveled. He chose to look beyond privilege, as he realized that until everyone is free, none can be free. So in the spirit of Nat Turner, Sojourner Truth, Toussaint L'Ouverture, Nanny, Cudjoe, Marcus Mosiah Garvey and his contemporary Malcolm X (El-Hajj Malik el-Shabazz), Martin Luther King chose to cast his lot with his brethren rather than enjoy the pleasures of sin for a season.

In the spirit of Dr. King, all of us ought to realize that we are accountable to our brothers and sisters. Like Dr. King, you too can become an overcomer. You can overcome the self-righteous feeling of elitism and indifference that causes many economically or academically successful brothers and sisters to adopt the "I've got mine now you get yours mentality." You can overcome the disease of self-hatred that continues to manifest itself in those among us who seek to assume the identity of the oppressor through their obsession with hair permanents, skin bleaches, and cosmetic surgery to straighten what God has flattened and deflate what God has inflated. Yes, in order to overcome, you must reject the Hakuna Matata philosophy that affects your accountability to others.

Accountability to God

Lastly, but by no means least, the Hakuna Matata philosophy negatively affects a person's sense of accountability to God. As Simba contemplated the words of Nala and wrestled with the decision to return home and face certain opposition from his Uncle Scar, he received a vision from his deceased father, Mufasa, who now resided in one of the heavenly luminaries. Simba, who bore an unmistakable resemblance to his father, was reminded that as long as he lived, he had a responsibility to elevate the standards of the ancestors.

While we may not share the theology that is inherent in the encounter between Simba and his father, one reality with which we have to come to terms concerns our accountability to God. Many of us with our Hakuna Matata attitudes have become so foolishly-brave that we feel we can get "in God's face" any time we want. Standards don't mean anything anymore. Those were for the old days. Who cares how short the skirt, tight the pants, low the neck-line, or high the waist line is? I know the Bible says we ought to dress modestly, but who cares? In your face, God!

This Hakuna Matata Philosophy also rejects the reality of our past as a people. By ignoring the divine mandates of our Creator, we manifest ingratitude to the "God of our weary years, the God of our silent tears, the God who has brought us thus far on our way." We forget so soon that "We have come over a way that with tears have been watered, We have come treading our way thro' the blood of the slaughtered." We forget that the same God who delivered Daniel and rescued the Hebrews from slavery in Egypt is the God who worked through Malcolm, Martin, Mugabe, and Mandella. As we look back on all that God has done for us, how dare we 'dis' Him with a Hakuna Matata philosophy? Now, more than ever, when doors of opportunities are opening for Black people at an unprecedented rate, we ought to be serving the God of our fathers and mothers with all of our heart, soul, strength and mind.

There ought to be more of us who are willing to follow the example of the recently deceased Noble Alexander, a Black Seventh-day Adventist pastor who was a political prisoner in Castro's Cuba.[4] His crime? Fidelity to the Almighty God. He could have denounced his faith and been released at any time. He could have opted for a lifestyle governed by Hakuna Matata—or, being in a communist nation, at least a modified version. But in spite of the beatings, the taunts and the torture, he chose to remain faithful to God. He knew that although his enemies could eventually kill him, if he remained faithful to death, he would receive the crown of life.

Like Pastor Alexander, more of us need to adopt the spirit of our ancestors and be willing to follow God all the way. While our colleagues are opting for the easy Hakuna Matata path with its compromise and apathy, we ought to be willing and ready to stand up and be counted. As Ellen White noted, "the greatest want in the world today is [still] the want of men [and women], men [and women] who will not be bought or sold; men [and women] who in their inmost souls are true and honest; men [and women] whose conscience is as true to duty as the needle to the pole; men [and women] who do not fear to call sin by its right name; men [and women] who will stand for the right though the heavens fall."[5] Yes! We need men and women who, when it comes to God, will not say Hakuna Matata, but rather, "What will you have me to do?"

Conclusion

In conclusion, if Christ has not been raised from the dead, then our responsibility to God, others, and self is at least optional and at the most inconsequential. But the majority of us who claim to be Christian profess to serve a risen Savior. We serve a Savior who, by the power of the Spirit, is able to make a difference in our lives. And so we realize that we cannot live our lives to the tune of Hakuna Matata. There is still a need to present our bodies as living sacrifices, holy, acceptable unto God (Rom 12:1). There is still a need to bear one another's burdens, and in so doing fulfill the law of Christ (Gal 6:2). There is still a need to recognize that we have been bought with a price so we ought to glorify God with our bodies (1 Cor 6:20).

At the end of the movie, the Lion King comes to himself and returns to his kingdom, where he rallies the forces to overcome the evil Scar and restore order into the Prideland. But this is fiction. What we face is reality. How will my story end? How will your story end? Will you be singing Hakuna Matata with the unconcerned masses when the cry goes out, "It is finished!" or will you be among those who have washed their robes in the blood of the Lamb. Will you hear the damning words "Depart from me I never knew you!" (Mt 25:41), or will you respond to the Savior's invitation: "Come ye blessed of my Father, inherit the kingdom prepared for you"? (Mt 25:34).

STUDY QUESTIONS

1. What is the central message of this chapter?

2. How does 1 Corinthians 15:32 remind us of our responsibility to self, others, and God?

3. What is your reaction to the author's claim that "every action has a reaction" (p. 40)? Why is it important to exercise discrimination in the things we watch or listen to for entertainment?

4. Many Black activists claim that Blacks have a responsibility to support the success of every Black business venture. Are we hurting or helping the Black community when we support celebrities who have low moral standards?

[Not only do many popular celebrities contribute to the problems that affect the stability of the Black community, but they often spend the bulk of their resources outside the community. Many of them play Black roles, but live in a European world.]

5. Maya Angelou tells of how she rose from a life of prostitution, abuse, and rejection, to become a powerful force in the neo-intellectual awakening of the twentieth century. How can Maya Angelou's life help you to establish goals that transcend your current condition?

6. Why is it essential for all Christian Black people to take a personal interest in the affairs of the Black community?

7. Name five practical things you can do to make a difference in your immediate community.

8. Dr. Martin Luther King, Jr. did not use his privileged

status in society to get lost in the suburbs of eurocentric apathy. How can Martin Luther King's life help you to make unselfish choices?

9.   Is there a relationship between one's responsibility to God, self, and neighbor? Consider Matthew 22:37-40 in your answer.

10.   Pastor Noble Alexander refused to succumb to persecution in Castro's Cuba. He realized that the accolades of humans are fickle and chose, rather, to place his confidence in the unshakable God. How can Pastor Alexander's life help you to resist the pressure to compromise principle for the sake of acceptance?

11.   Make a list of the five most important lessons you have learned from this chapter.

12.   Reflect on how this chapter has affected you as a person.

13.   Evaluate how this chapter has affected your relationship with God.

CHAPTER FIVE

WORLDLY WINE AND A PERISHING PEOPLE

Fallen, fallen is Babylon the great!
She has made all nations drink of the
wine of the wrath of her fornication.
(Revelation 14:8)

J ames Weldon Johnson's "Lift Every Voice and Sing,"[1] the national anthem of the African-American, and indeed of diasporic Africans and African nationals in all places, epitomizes the African experience. It encourages us as a people to continue singing in one voice until the entire earth "rings with the harmony of liberty." It reminds us, "We have come over a way that with tears have been watered, We have come treading our way thro' the blood of the slaughtered." And then we are reminded that the one who has brought us through is the "God of our weary years, God of our silent tears."

However, the lines in this anthem that probably speak most to us in this age characterized by narcissistic-secularism are those that warn us: "Lest our feet stray from the places, our God, where we met Thee, Lest our hearts, drunk with the wine of the world, we forget thee." They speak loudly to us at this time, because the spiritual experience of the African in America is being attacked from a number of angles, and the foundation on which our faith is built is gradually being eroded.

We must face the reality that the threats that impinge upon the survivability of African-American spirituality are to be seen both as the cause and the result of the problem. These two extremities are brought into tension when we confront the fact that the devil is upset with anyone who places trust and faith in God. Indeed, in his discussion about the great war between good and evil forces, John writes, "the Dragon was angry with the woman, and went to make war with the remnant of her seed who keep the commandments of God and bear testimony to Jesus" (Rev 12:19).

The devil is angry with Black people because in spite of the fiery arrows that he shoots at us, we refuse to give up our faith in God. Instead of hoisting the white flag of surrender, we frustrate his efforts by singing, "I don't feel no ways tired, I've come too far from where I started from, Nobody told me that the road would be easy, I don't believe he brought me this far to leave me!"[2] We know that the road ahead will also have its challenges, but we move forward knowing, "We have nothing to fear for the future, except as we shall forget the way the Lord has led us, and His teaching in our past history."[3] In spite of our resilience, the devil continues his attempts to make us fearful. In this chapter, we will briefly look at what I perceive to be the four major threats to the survivability of African-American spirituality.

Gradual Erosion of Family and Community

The first major threat is manifest in the gradual erosion of the Black family and community. We may want to look at the government for someone to blame, and criticize those who want to cut back on welfare aid to the poor and underprivileged. However, the biggest threat to the Black community is not the "man." The biggest menace is not the government. We are to blame for our community ills. The old proverb states: "A house divided among itself cannot stand." Unfortunately, while we are busy criticizing the divide and conquer policies of the White House and Congress, our own Black house is in disarray. And we are so caught up in our dishonest state of denial that we refuse to come together. With pitiful self-deprecation we have accepted the status assigned to us by a racist society and have mastered the art of keeping ourselves in oppressive bondage.

We recognize that we are some of the most mixed up people in the world—our foremothers having been raped continually by the massa. We also recognize that our heritage is one built on single-parent families when the massa refused to acknowledge us as his offspring, but preferred to view us as his property. Nonetheless, as a people its about time that we came to terms with the fact that the Emancipation Proclamation was heralded over one-hundred-and-forty years ago. It's about time that we started to live like free people. Instead of making the most of our limited freedom, too many of our people have chosen to remain in mental slavery. How else can you explain the millions of males (not necessarily "men") among us who imitate the callous slave master and father children out of wedlock. And after they have sown their wild oats, most of these stud machines don't even give a care about the welfare of their offspring or the mothers who bore them. As a result, recent statistics show that 68% of black children are born out of wedlock, while 50% of black homes are led by single, unmarried women.

We have become our own worst enemy. We live in an age when we have to fear our own people more than we do the Ku Klux Klan. It is no secret that a brother is six times more likely to be killed by another brother than by a White man.

So serious is the problem of Black on Black crime in our communities that one million Black men are currently incarcerated. Somewhere in our trek from slavery to liberation, the devil has managed to usurp control over our communities, and we have apparently handed him the keys to our freedom.

Many of us have also been influenced by the minstrel mentality and feel that our lot in life is to entertain the masses. And what sells? Sex and crudeness. The desire to satisfy the hedonistic appetite of post-modern society is so strong that the major television network that claims to represent Blacks does very little to elevate the consciousness of our people. Instead, it is geared towards the tantalizing appetite of consumerism. Furthermore, the television serials that purport to highlight Black life often reinforce the stereotypical images of the majority culture. We have become so accustomed to celebrating the negative, that some of our own thinkers even attacked Bill Cosby when he dared to chastise the community for its lapsed morals and its comfort with mediocrity.[4]

What message are our children getting about what it means to be Black? Are they to grow up thinking that being Black means to curse like Chris Rock, Eddie Murphy and Richard Pryor? Are they going to emulate the sex-ploits of Coby Bryant and Jesse Jackson or the gangsta mentality of Ron Artest and Mike Tyson? Not if we do something about it! They must learn that they are not predisposed to living a life of reckless immorality. They must be shown that there is another way to live. They must be presented with role models who utter pure speech, live chaste lives, and know how to control their tempers. They must be continually reminded that the freedom of our people was effected by an unbending faith in a mighty God who calls us all to spiritual accountability.

Another failure in the Black community stems from our departure from the African ideal of "one village one child." There used to be a time when we had to respect all elders in the community. These elders were as authoritative as our very own parents. If we were seen misbehaving on the streets, we would expect to be soundly reprimanded by the disciplining elder. And when our parents received the news, we knew exactly what to expect when we got home. However, it's not like this anymore, since many of those who are most likely to transmit the standards have deserted our communities. When we achieve our college degrees and professional certifications, we make a quick exodus to the suburbs and only go back to the ghetto to gather information for the lecture circuit so that we can capitalize on the misfortunes of our people. We no longer live out our parents' convictions that "We are our brothers' and sisters' keepers." The devil has sunken his teeth into our families and communities and has inauspiciously affected the spirituality which once girded our common loyalty.

Liberal European Theology

A second threat to the survivability of Black spirituality is the liberal European theology that permeates the mainline seminaries and has infiltrated our pulpits all around the world. This theology basically tries to find meaning in myth as it relegates the scriptures to the level of Aesop's fables, or the fairy stories upon which we were raised. As such, the biblical stories are said to be "truth" not in the historical sense, but in the sense that the message entailed is true of the human situation. Consequently, the accounts in the Bible become etiological and mythic in nature—a mere reflection of the imaginations of those who sought to construct a history for themselves.

I dare say that such an approach to the scriptures is a direct affront to the Black Experience not only here in America, but throughout the African diaspora where Black people have relied on these stories to sustain their hope. The very basis of our hope for freedom was the Exodus story. On more than one occasion, we invoked the spirit of Moses as we sang: "Go down Moses, way down in Egypt land, tell ole Pharaoh, 'Let my people go.'" When we contemplate how God has worked with us, we cannot accept Norman Gottwald's theory that the tribes of Israel were rebellious Canaanites and not emancipated slaves. We reject these theories because we believe that God delivered Israel from oppression in the land of the enemy. We believe that God is responsible for lifting the oppressor's yoke. In fact, many of our ancestors were encouraged with the historical assurance: "Didn't my Lord deliver Daniel? Then why not every man?" Neither can we follow European skeptics in denying the possibility of miracles and the supernatural working of the Holy Spirit, for many of us have personally encountered the Spirit or know someone who has been "slain" by the Spirit.

The tenets of liberal European theology also attack those divine standards of morality that have governed our society. We have always been a graceful people who even reach out to those among us who have crossed our socially defined boundaries. We don't reject family members who birth out of wedlock, struggle with sexual identity or get hooked on addictive drugs. However, at the same time we have always been careful to differentiate between righteous living and sin. Our spiritual awareness has made us conscious of the reality that God's Word is a lamp unto our feet and a light unto our path (Ps 119:150). We are thankful for the price that Jesus has paid for us on the cross, and so we pledge to live in harmony with His Word.

One of our songs asks the questions: "What shall I render unto God for all his mercies? What shall I render, What shall I give?"[5] Then the answer is given in the second verse: "All I can render is my body and my soul. That's all I can render, That's all I can give." We cannot sing these songs with meaning if we hold unto the humanistic theology as propounded by liberal Europeans. We cannot lift our voice in spiritual confession if we are living on the "down low." Like Paul, we "harden our bodies with blows" (1 Cor 9:27) and learn the discipline of denial. Its not an easy struggle, but we forge forward knowing that one day we will receive our reward and resound the rapturous anthem: "How I got over, How I got over, Oh, my soul looks back and wonders how I got over!"[6]

Exploitation by Our Spiritual Leaders

A third factor that threatens to corrode the spirituality of the African in America is the corruption that is rampant among our spiritual leaders. From the days of slavery, the preacher was the most powerful figure in the Black community. The powerful mystique of the Black preacher has remained to this very day. This status should come with great moral responsibility. However, the opposite is too often the case. In many ways, our spiritual leaders have taken on the personae of the gods in the Greek pantheon who are exempt from the moral laws that govern human relationships. Members are often so hypnotized by clergy charisma that they would dismiss the deacon for cussing under his breath before they reprimand the reverend for embezzling the funds.

Many Black ministers have been spoiled and know how easy it is for the power of the office to contaminate them. Some are so infused with hubris that they believe they are excused from practicing what they preach. Pastoral ministry for many has become a way to merit instant prestige and unparalleled flexibility. This abomination must stop! Preachers need to stop hiding behind their human frailties and start relying on their divine accessibility. It is true that those who are called to ministry are not granted instant immunity from temptation; however, God does not call anyone whom he does not equip with the spiritual power to overcome. All ministers should be able and willing to elevate themselves as paradigms of Christ. However, this will only happen when they realize that just like the members to whom they preach, "They've got to walk that lonesome valley, they've got to walk it by themselves, and no-one else can walk it for them, they've got to walk it by themselves."

Further, our Black ministers cannot continue to exploit the many people who have become hopelessly gullible in their quest to be in the presence of a wonder-working *savior*. My blood boils when I think of celebrity ministers living in kingly opulence supported by the blood, sweat and tears of the desperate faithful who are already swamped by consumer debt. With hardened hearts, they prey on those who pray, extort those who exalt, and feed fallacious hype to those who fervently hope. Having mastered the fine art of religious manipulation, many of our preachers have been fashioned into cult icons by the same people who look to them for guidance and support. Why is it that so many of our people followed

Jim Jones to their death in Jonestown, Guyana? Why is it that so many were consumed in the fire that blazed through the Branch Davidian compound in Waco, Texas?

If our people don't learn that true spirituality is not derived from an esoteric leader but comes from a faith in an unfailing God, then the Church which is the symbol of Black spirituality will begin to crumble as the children of those who have been exploited "wise up" and assimilate themselves into the secularism of the larger society. If our leaders are not held accountable, the very institution that offered stability and direction will disintegrate into oblivion. If we do not arise from the drunken slumber that is brought about by our fascination with the world's wine, we will forget the very God who can sober us as we fall into the lair of the enemy of God's people.

Conflict Over Church and Community
The final threat to the survivability of the spirituality of the African in America arises from the conflicting views regarding the role of the church in the community. We often find that there are two extremes to this threat. The first is the view that the church is to act as an agent of social change in society. This view, built upon liberation theologies as propounded by the likes of Jurgen Möltmann and Gustavo Gutierrez, often places little emphasis on the need for personal salvation and a personal relationship with Jesus Christ. Instead, there is a strong emphasis on the desire to transform whole communities at once. Please don't get me wrong. This is indeed a noble ideal, and it would be wonderful if societal change could be effected *en masse*. However, thousands of years of experience has taught us that change cannot come about through legislation.

Those of us who have been on the societal battlefield have had to come to terms with the nature of our spiritual warfare. Through experience we have learned that societies are altered one life at a time as willing individuals acknowledge their shortcomings and seek transformation. We have come to accept that our soup kitchens, homeless shelters and after-school tutoring services are nothing if they are not grounded in the ministry of the Holy Spirit. Our mission is not accomplished when we satisfy the people's physical hunger. It is only complete when they are introduced to the true Source of their bread. Our acts of kindness should not merely focus on people coming to church for a warm meal, but should be intentional in tuning their hearts and minds to respond to the Christ who stands at the door and knocks. The church *should* be an agent of change in the community, but the transformation should be more than social—it must be spiritual.

While some of our spiritual communities have become extensions of government social service agencies, others have become so heavenly minded that they are no earthly good. Some of our churches are so concerned with holiness that they don't want to get contaminated by helping the heathen. It's almost as if they feel that church life insulates and isolates them from the community. A growing number of people who attend inner city churches have long since left the neighborhood and have no intimate concern for those who live within the boundaries of their parishes.

Those whose spiritual lives are strictly limited to church attendance will do well to heed the words of Jesse Jackson, who proclaimed, "I would rather have dirty hands and a clean heart, than clean hands and a dirty heart." Many in our churches have chosen to keep their hands clean and do not take the time to reason that the Holy Spirit who stirs Sister Wright to jump and shout on Sunday is not the same spirit that possesses her husband to beat her when she comes home from church. They have not taken the opportunity to move beyond contributing to the missions fund and start involving themselves in mission activities. They have not learned to move out of church committee meetings and commit themselves to serving as mentors for directionless youth. It's time we stopped simply saying "I'll pray for you" and started doing something about the problems that plague our communities. But in order for the role of the church to remain valid and our spirituality to remain authentic, our social outreach must always be informed by our commitment to God and to His word.

Conclusion

In conclusion, I would like to offer four ways in which we can help our communities resist the demonic attacks I have highlighted in this chapter. The first is found in the words of the late Bob Marley, who in his "Redemption Song" penned the words: "Emancipate yourselves from mental slavery, none but ourselves can free our minds." Until we shake off the destructive legacy inherited from slavery that causes us to rape and kill in the pattern of our former owners, we will never realize our full spiritual potential.

Secondly, there is a need for us to hold our spiritual leaders accountable. Those who claim to have been called by God to lead His people should not be allowed to exploit those who have been entrusted to their care. "To whom much is given, much is required" (Lk 12:48).

Thirdly, there is a continuous need for an affirmation of God's acts in history and the surety of His promises. We need to remember that the same God who has led us in the past will continue to lead us in the future. "Didn't my Lord deliver Daniel?"

Finally, there needs to be an affirmation of the central role of the Church in our communities. As representatives of Jesus Christ, we need to let our lights shine in this dark and evil age in which we live. Join me in the campaign against the worldly wine that is slowly transforming us into a perishing people.

Study Questions

1. What is the central message of this chapter?

2. Carefully analyze the words in the second verse of "Lift Every Voice and Sing." What is the warning cry in these verses?

3. In light of Revelation 14:8, why is it so imperative for Black Christians to resist the Babylonian wine that permeates society?

4. What is your reaction to the author's claim that "we live in an age in which we fear our own people more than we do the Ku Klux Klan?"

5. To what extent does the Black entertainment industry influence the Black community? Think of the last five Black movies you have watched. How would you evaluate the moral value of each of these movies?

6. Why do so many Black entertainers thrive on immorality? As Christians, how does Philippians 4:8 help us to respond to those elements of the Black entertainment industry that promote ungodly values?

7. If the biblical stories in the scriptures are myths, as liberal European theology charges, what hope do we have as a people?

[The scriptures give us hope for the past, present, and future. From the perspective of the past, it is somewhat comforting to know that the injustices our ancestors experienced will be avenged. The present power of the word allows us to affirm our self-worth as children of God, and empowers us to forgive those who are repentant for—or ignorant of—their sins against us. The scriptures also affirm the surety of our future when we finally realize our true status as sons and daughters of God.]

8.   Carefully analyze Jeremiah 23:1-4. What responsibility does the spiritual leader have to the people under his or her care? To whom is the leader accountable?

9.   Does the fact that there are hypocritical and exploitative spiritual leaders provide an excuse for Blacks to reject Christianity? Why, or why not?

[Corrupt leaders can be found in all faith communities. Aware of this anomaly and in touch with his own fallibility, the apostle Paul charges the Corinthians to follow him, but only as long as he follows Christ (1 Cor 11:1). The moment he strays from the path or abuses his authority, he has forfeited his right to lead.]

10.   Why is it so important to elevate Jesus in our community involvement?

11.   How does the parable of the Final Judgement in Matthew 25:31-46 address the need for Black Christians to experience an inner righteousness that moves them from the pews to the mission fields in our communities?

12.   Make a list of the five most important lessons you have learned from this chapter.

13.   Reflect on how this chapter has affected you as a person.

14.   Evaluate how this chapter has affected your relationship with God.

CHAPTER SIX

"WE SHALL OVERCOME"

*To the one who conquers, I will give a place with me
on my throne, just as I myself conquered and sat
down with my father on his throne.*
(Revelation 3:21)

The Greek word, Laodicea, means "a people being judged." As I reflect on the notion of a judged people, I am reminded that many have interpreted the past four centuries of persecution and suffering as evidence that African people are under judgement. These beliefs have been inculcated into the global psyche to such an extent that many of our own believe we are under Divine punishment. We have been tried in the international court of injustice and found guilty of a crime that nobody seems to be able to identify. As a result, we have been sentenced—it seems—to a lifetime of hard labor without the possibility of parole.

Our primary condemners originated in Europe. They came
to our homeland with their corrupting influences and muscled
themselves into power. They forced us into second class
citizenship in our own nations, as they raped and pillaged the
land, taking away the natural resources to finance the
industrialization of Europe and America. They disregarded the
contribution that African universities of antiquity had made to
science, medicine, and mathematics.[1] They ignored the
organized way in which we dealt with tribal conflict. They
were unaware that ours was a nation where the majority of
the people shared a belief in one God, and numerous tribes
were monotheistic Sabbatarians long before the missionaries
came.[2] All of our accomplishments were overlooked as our
oppressors chose to treat us as if we were sub-human.

No other group of people in recent history has suffered as
long and intensely as Blacks. I do not wish to belittle the horror
of the atrocities endured by European Jews under the cruel
regime of Adolf Hitler's *Dritte Reich*. During their period of
affliction, six million men, women and children were extermi-
nated from the human race. However, the intense portion of
their atrocity only lasted for six years. This is less than one
fifth of one percent of the time that Blacks have suffered on
an international scale. Further, at the end of their period of
suffering, the Jews were appeased with a homeland when the
United Nations callously displaced innocent Palestinians in
Hitler-like fashion.

Unlike their Jewish siblings in suffering, Blacks have never
been compensated for their pain. Like Israel of old, we have
been forced to work under hard taskmasters who continuously
command us to make bricks without straw. Our women have
been raped, our men have been lynched, and our children
have been taken away from us in their infancy. It is no wonder
that many have accepted the racist theory that we are a
cursed race and are suffering the consequences of Ham's sin.
It is no puzzle to see why so many bigots look at our suffering
as a judgment from God.

With this history of accusation and suspicion, all would
have to admit that the Black nation does indeed bear the

name "Laodicea." However, the judgement that we experience is not a judgement from God, but a pre-judgement from oppressive humans. We have been—and still are—victims of prejudice as the oppressors choose to draw certain conclusions about us before they become acquainted with the facts. To the oppressor we were only three-fifths human, so the constitution that granted "freedom" and "liberty" to all did not apply to us. To the oppressor, we lacked intelligence, so we were not given the opportunity to go to school. To the oppressor, we came from primitive civilizations, so we were supposed to be content with living in inferior and dehumanizing conditions eating corn bread, collard greens and chitterlings. To the oppressor, we are born to fail, so a blind eye is turned to the illegal drugs and weapons that keep on pouring into our neighborhoods. To put it bluntly, we are continually being prejudged.

A Better Tomorrow

In an effort to keep us servile, this nation has given us an opportunity to have a month dedicated to the remembrance of our history. For the past decade or so, our celebration has taken on new meaning following the release of Nelson Mandela from political imprisonment on February 18, 1990. His timely release indicated a softening of heart of the South African government under F. W. De Klerk, who slowly came to the realization that regardless of skin color, we are all God's children. And even as we observe the liberation that permeates through the Azanian Nation, our minds go back to the civil rights struggle that took place in this very nation. In fact, Blacks in South Africa and the United States of America were involved in the quest for equality at the same time. The late fifties and early sixties not only saw peaceful protests by the Southern Christian Leadership Conference and the National Association for the Advancement of Colored People on the streets of America, but also in South Africa the African National Congress (ANC) and Pan African Congress (PAC) were very much in solidarity with those of us who reside in the Americas.

Even as we reflect on those days, we remember how the

struggle in South Africa was halted after the dreaded Sharpeville Massacre, which resulted in the death of seventy innocent Black Africans—including women and children—and the mutilation of thousands of others. We remember how after this terrible massacre, the ANC gave up its peaceful protest efforts and declared war against the government. We remember how Nelson Mandela offered a symbol of hope to his people as he appeared as a Moses—one drawn from among the people. We remember how this Moses was arrested and tried for treason, then sentenced to a life term in prison on the notorious Robben Island. We also remember how after twenty seven years in captivity, Mandela emerged older and wiser, but still cognizant of his duty as a Moses—still prepared to lead his people to liberation. Mandela realized that if God had intended for a people to remain in slavery, he would never have led Israel out of Egypt.

In the face of seemingly insurmountable obstacles, Mandela was able to lead his people across the tumultuous Jordan. He stands taller today as the first democratically elected leader of that fabricated nation. The years of toil and tenacity appear to have paid off, as the people of Azania have overcome the seemingly impossible.

As I rejoice with Mandela and the people of Azania, my mind rushes to another Black Moses. This Moses was born in a different hemisphere on Tuesday January 15, 1929. He seemed to be just another Black baby born in the cruel and vicious South. Destined to a life of hatred and oppression, this Black baby was to show the world what it meant to overcome. He managed to overcome the segregated educational system when he entered Morehouse College at the age of fifteen and received his doctorate in Systematic Theology by the age of twenty-five. He managed to overcome career counseling pressure when he recognized that his true calling was to the gospel ministry and not to Sociology. He managed to overcome hatred when he calmed down an angry mob who had gathered to avenge the bombing of his house. He managed to overcome the unjust judiciary system of the United States when he was acquitted of trumped-up perjury charges, and released on bail on countless occasions. He managed to overcome tradition when he spearheaded the campaign that led to the passing of the Civil Rights Act. He managed to overcome fear when he prophesied his death, expressing the desire for longevity, but prepared to do God's will and suffer the consequences so that others may feast on the milk and honey in the Promised Land that he saw beyond the mountain-top.

The theme of the Civil Rights struggle and a memory text as familiar as the Lord's Prayer in the home of every American Black is the song "We shall overcome." This anthem has been an inspiration to millions of Blacks in the United States and around the globe. However, it is now more that thirty years since the song was adopted, and racism is still a reality in America. According to some estimates, Blacks comprise 75% of the prison population and earn just 60% of the average salary of our white counterparts. We continue to receive inferior education in the inner cities, where we are housed in reservations known as Government Housing Projects. We are continually confronted with presidents who feels that it is more profitable to put tax payers' money into the military than in education.

Having said all this, I must hasten to give credit where it is due. All is not dismal. In spite of the negative side of the Black community that the media enjoys to highlight, we do see some progress. Many Blacks now occupy prestigious upper-level positions, both in public and private sectors. Many, like George Jefferson, have "moved on up to the East Side and finally got a piece of the pie." Nonetheless, even with all of these images of success, we still have to ask the question "Have we really overcome?" Many who have attained success—in worldly standards—have forgotten from whence they have come. A growing number of Black professionals have confused progress with the acquisition of European cars, clothes, designer watches, and spouses. Please don't misunderstand me. I am not against interracial relationships; I just have a problem with those who equate success with total assimilation into the majority culture to the detriment of the culture that nurtured them. With the increase in "Black flight," we are experiencing a corrupted version of William Dubois'

philosophy—a "talented tenth" of Black, educated professionals while the majority still wallow in the injustices of the system.

An Analysis of the Phrase

The current dilemma of Blacks in the United States and
around the globe has forced me to delve into a critical
exegesis of the phrase "We shall overcome" as propounded
by Martin Luther King and the freedom movement of the
sixties. The first word, "we," denotes unity. In the context of
this phrase, the "we" refers directly to a people, a Black
people. The "we" in the phrase means more that just a mere
association of the people involved, for a people can be
associated but still not have the same aim. The "we" involves
a concerted effort of togetherness in purpose. It is a militantly
determined "we." Once the "we" is fully defined, it will
correctly be rendered as "We As One."

The second word in the phrase, "shall," expresses a
determined positiveness. It doesn't share the uncertainty
associated with the subjunctive terms "might" or "maybe." It is
indicative of reality—a proleptic expression. It is a term that is
full of itself—full of pomp and audacity. Nothing can get in the
way of shall. You can set up the roadblock of Plessy versus
Ferguson, but "shall" responds with Brown versus the Board of
Education. You can set up the roadblock of selective ethnically
motivated nepotism, but "shall" responds with Affirmative
Action. You can set up the roadblock of a Mark Fuhrman, but
shall responds with a Johnny Cochrane. Yes, "shall" is a
futuristic term, but it is certain of itself.

The third word in this triumvirate is "overcome." "Overcome" is a compound construction of the verb "come" and the
preposition "over." The very use of this word suggests that we
are involved in a struggle, but refuse to give up because we
know "it ain't over 'til its over." It may seem as if we are
down, but we are not yet out. The armies of European
oppression may be attacking us with their weapons of
warfare, but we are a resilient people who refuse to back
down in the face of adversity. We were supposed to be dead
a long time ago, having been brought from a tropical climate
and forced to live in drafty shacks in the harsh winters of the

United States, but we refused to give up. This tenacious attitude undergirds our understanding of "overcome," for despite all odds we see an "overwhelming victory." With this in mind, the entire phrase "We shall overcome" can be rendered in finality as "We as one shall definitely gain an overwhelming victory."

This understanding of the phrase expresses a positive action. However, in a massive confusion over the meaning of "we," some of our compatriots feel that their overcoming does not mean that they should help their brothers or sisters who have not reached as high up the acceptance ladder as they, and these confused individuals have transformed the active theme of the Black struggle into a passive threat. Consequently, the term "we shall overcome" now means for some "we shall *be* overcome."

The Reality of Our Situation

The difference in these two statements is not simply in the change of voice from active to passive, but it lies in the "we." Indeed, the old adage states, "United we stand, Divided we fall"—"United *we as one* stand" as opposed to "Divided *we as individuals* fall." The "We as one" encompasses more that just the Black inhabitants of this nation, but every Black person on the face of the globe. Regardless of where we may find ourselves socially or politically, it behooves us to remain in solidarity with our suffering brothers and sisters. Marcus Garvey and The Universal Negro Improvement Association captured this idea when they pushed for a united Negro nation. Indeed, King's famous speech on the night before the assassin's bullet ripped through his chest included the statement:

> We've got some difficult days ahead. But it doesn't matter with me now. Because I have been to the mountaintop.... Like anybody, I would like to live a long life; longevity has its place. But I'm not concerned about that now. I just want to do God's will. And He has allowed me to go to the mountain. And I've looked over. And I've seen the Promised Land. I may not get there with you, but I want you to know that we *as a*

people will get to the Promised Land.

Notice that Dr. King said "We as a people." Not "We as African Americans," or "We as Bahamians," or "We as Barbadians," or "We as Trinadadians," or "We as Azanians" or "We as Liberians," but "We *as a people* will get to the Promised Land."

And even as we examine the articulated vision of Dr. King when he stood before the huddled masses who gathered at the National Mall during the celebrated March on Washington for Jobs and Freedom in 1963, we see his emphasis on the necessity for a United Negro Front: "I have a dream that one day on the red hills of Georgia, the sons of former slaves and the sons of former slave owners will be able to sit down together at the table of brotherhood." But I am here to say today, that before we can sit down with the sons of former slave owners, we must learn to sit down with the sons of former slaves. Before we strive to overcome the discrimination, oppression, retribution, and condemnation inflicted by the sons of former slave owners, we must learn to overcome the discrimination, oppression, retribution. and condemnation imposed by the sons of former slaves.

As I reflect on the disunity in the Black community, I am forced to concede that Martin Luther King's joy would not have been complete if he were alive today. Indeed, it was a united and not a disoriented people who boycotted the buses in Motgomery, Alabama from December 1955 to November 1956 after Mrs. Rosa Parks refused to obey an unjust law. It was a united and not a disoriented people who were attacked by dogs and high power fire hoses when the notorious Sheriff Bull Connors tried to quench their zeal. It was a united and not a disoriented people who marched on Washington pressing for their rights on August 28, 1963. It was a united and not a disoriented people who stood behind the 1964 Civil Rights Acts that promised equal rights for *all* American citizens. It was a united and not a disoriented people who mourned for Dr. King in 1968 after he was assassinated at the youthful age of thirty-nine. Looking back at these expressions of unity, I am forced to say that King's joy would not be complete with our status today.

However, Dr. King may not have been altogether disheartened, for being a minister of the gospel he should have known that his ultimate dream of sons of slaves and slave owners sitting in unity may only be possible in glory. In spite of the benefits that may be afforded by this country, it is still not the Promised Land. Nonetheless, Dr. King did expect those of us who dream with him to at least attempt to make a difference in this unjust world.

Conclusion: The Solution to Our Problem

Lerome Bennett, Jr. asks the question in the January 1986 issue of "Ebony Magazine":

What are we doing, and what are we prepared to do to insure that King did not dream and die in vain? And if he could speak to us... from his living grave, he would tell us that nothing can stop us here if we keep the faith of our fathers and mothers and walk together and dream together.

Yes, my fellow dreamers, only if we keep the faith of our fathers and mothers can we overcome.

Nonetheless, as a Christian people, we realize that even more important than the fight against racism and Black on Black expressions of self hatred is the fight against our sinful selves. It may have been this reality that inspired George Benson to pen the words: "The greatest love of all is the need to love yourself." Self love is indeed as equally important as the love for God and neighbor (Lk 10:27). If you truly love yourself, you would understand what Dr. King meant when he said that every man, woman, and child is responsible for his or her own freedom. It is only when every man, woman, and child finds the secret of overcoming self that we will have a chance of overcoming as a people.

When we overcome self, we will be better prepared—by the grace of God—to liberate humanity as we present to them a way in which they too can overcome self. Dr. King realized that to overcome meant to surrender completely to God and hide self behind the cross of Jesus. Although we as a people need to overcome on this earth and gain freedom from the oppressive forces of capitalism and neo-Apartheid, our ultimate aim should be to overcome the obstacles that stand between us and the kingdom of the Almighty God.

As we contemplate our quest to overcome, the Word of God gives us hope for today. Indeed in his letter to the seven churches, Jesus through John the Revelator has offered several promises that will keep us going. Some of you like the members of the church in Ephesus may be hungry now. You may be among the millions of unemployed or underemployed. You find it difficult to pay the bills, and always have more month left at the end of your money. You know what it is like to do without and go to bed hungry. If you fit this category, Jesus promises that "the one who overcomes will eat of the tree of life which is in the paradise of God" (Rev 2:7).

Or you may be like those in Smyrna who are persecuted for their faith. You may even have suffered persecution simply because others perceive that you inherited the "wrong" pigmentation. There may even be some who place their lives in mortal danger every time they leave their homes and step into the battleground of a neighborhood besieged by rival gangs. If you are among those whose living environment has forced you on the list of endangered species, Jesus promises that if you overcome "you will not be harmed in the second death" (Rev 2:11).

Or, like many in the church of Pergamos, you may be tired of living in the shadow of past injustices. You may have engaged in genealogical research with the hope of duplicating Alex Haley's success, but cannot research beyond three generations of ancestors. You are the unwilling recipient of a slave name that constantly reminds you of your fragmented past—a name that continually reminds you that your ancestors were once somebody's property. But you don't have to file a petition at the Social Security office for a name change. You don't have to swap your European slave name for an Arabic slave name. For Jesus has promised that all who overcome will receive a white stone, "and on that stone is written a new name that is known to none but the recipient" (Rev 2:17). "There's a new name written in glory, and it's mine!"

Or, like the brethren in Thyatira, you may be living in a society that has deprived you of your rights. Justice for the powerful ruling class means "just us," and there is nobody who is willing to advocate your cause. Politicians are infected with the virus of corruption and law enforcement officers abuse their authority. If you dare to confront the system, you will be silenced by terrorist assassins financed from the government's coffers. And if they mistake you for an Arab, you may just end up with the abused detainees at Guantanamo Bay. But even as you live in fear of the authorities, Jesus vows that the one who overcomes and maintains faith, will be given "authority over the nations to rule them with an iron rod similar to when clay pots are broken in pieces" (Rev 2:26-27).

Or, like those in Sardis, you may be among the untouchables in Western society. As if controlled by a Hindu-inspired classism, society has relegated you to the bottom rungs of the social ladder. Your contributions to science and technology have been conveniently forgotten or deceptively credited to a person of "respectable" pedigree. In spite of the efforts of Jesse Jackson, Carol Mosely-Braun, Shirley Chisholm and Al Sharpton, you may never see a Black leader in the White House. In the spirit of polite tokenism the occasional person of color may be paraded in the national spotlight, but the field of politics and business are still limited to those who enter "by invitation only." But don't despair, for Jesus pledges that all who overcome will be clothed in sparkling designer garments, and their names will be included in the only invitation list that counts—the Book of Life (Rev 3:5).

Or, like those in Philadelphia, you may be trying to find your place in life. For some strange reason, you just don't seem to fit in. You are ostracized on the job because of your ethical integrity. Unfortunately, you are also pushed aside at your church because you dare to call the leaders to accountability. You are fed up with the deceitful habits of those worldly hypocrites who parade as saints on the weekends. You have moved from church to church and have still not found a place where the transforming Spirit dwells. To you, Jesus affirms that if you overcome, He "will make you a steadfast pillar in the temple of his God, and you will never go out of it" (Rev 3:12).

Or, you may even be like those in the Church of Laodecia.

You have engaged in a ferocious battle against sin and lukewarmness. You have experienced the disappointment of caving to the weight of peer pressure. You know what it means to be distracted from the path of holiness. But through it all, you have determined to hold on to the anchored rope that will help you to surmount the rough side of the mountain. Even as you read this book, you may be considering throwing in the towel, but Jesus urges you to look forward and not back. He encourages you to focus on your future and not your past. He bids you to meditate on your victories and not your failures. He challenges you to vision the prize and not get distracted by the struggle. He offers you the ultimate reward with the words, "The one who overcomes will be given an opportunity to share my throne, just as I overcame and had the privilege of sharing my Father's throne" (Rev 3:21).

With these wonderful promises to spur me on, I don't know about you, but I am determined to overcome. Not just in temporal matters, but in those matters pertaining to my eternal life. Join me as together we pick up the spirit of the freedom movement and march towards that new day when our song will not be "We shall overcome," but "We have overcome."

STUDY QUESTIONS

1.   What is the central message of this chapter?

2.   How has the myth of the "Curse of Ham" contributed to the suffering of Black people? According to Genesis 9:18-29, was Ham really cursed?

[The myth of the "Curse of Ham" is the biggest lie in Eurocentric Christianity. The text plainly states that it was not Ham, but Canaan, his son, who was cursed by Noah. This curse is actually a prophecy of Israel's eventual occupation of the land of Canaan. No curse is placed on the dark skinned inhabitants of Cush (Ethiopia) or Mizraim (Egypt).]

3.   What is your response to the author's claim that Black

people bear the name "Laodicea"? How should Black people respond to prejudice?

[The best way to respond to prejudice is by refuting the misconceptions through our actions. Ben Carson, Mae Jemison, Tiger Woods, Elijah McKoy, Ron Brown, and a host of others, have all demonstrated that Black people have as much intellectual and creative abilities as people from any other ethnic group.]

4.   List ten similarities between the life of Moses, and the lives of Nelson Mandella, Martin Luther King, Jr., and Malcolm X.

5.   Why does God appoint visible leaders to lead struggles for freedom? Do you believe that Mandella, Martin, and Malcolm carried God's endorsement? (Please discard your theological biases as you respond to this question.)

6.   What does it mean to "overcome"? What is your assessment of the author's analysis of the phrase "We Shall Overcome"? Can Black people experience true victory if they are not united in purpose?

7.   In Revelation 2 and 3, "overcome" is a translation of the Greek word, *nikeo*, which means "to be victorious." The term assumes that the one who needs to overcome is engaged in warfare and must defeat the enemy. The biggest challenge for Black people is defining the enemy. Many conclude that the enemy is the White man. According to Ephesians 6:10-12, can Black people really claim that the *White man* is the enemy?

[After preaching Elijah Muhammad's doctrine that the White man is the devil, Malcolm X's trip to Mecca made him realize that the problem was bigger than the white man. There are good and bad people in all ethnic groups.]

8.   Why is it important for Black people to identify with Black suffering in whatever country it occurs?

[Although there may be different symptoms of Black global oppression, the cause is the same. The eurocentric West is responsible for creating the societal viruses that have affected Black communities around the globe. These viruses have not only manifested themselves through slavery, but also through imperialistic colonization. In showing solidarity with the suffering of Blacks around the globe, we recognize the common source of the problem. In adapting a position of apathy, we become a part of the problem. Desmond Tutu once said to those countries claiming to be neutral towards Apartheid South Africa, "If an elephant is standing on the foot of a mouse and you say you are neutral, the mouse would not appreciate your neutrality."]

9.   Do you really think it is possible for Black people to experience full liberation and equality in the foreseeable future?

10. Analyze the author's application of the messages to the seven churches in Revelation 2:1-3:22. Which three messages do you find the most helpful in establishing your hope for a better tomorrow?

11. Make a list of the five most important lessons you have learned from this chapter.

12. Reflect on how this chapter has affected you as a person.

13. Evaluate how this chapter has affected your relationship with God.

CHAPTER SEVEN

ONE VILLAGE, ONE CHILD

All who believed were together and held all things in common;
they would sell their possessions and goods and distribute
their proceeds to all, as they had need.
(Acts 2:44-45)

In this age of rebellion, it has become customary for people to stress their individuality. In a bid to show how independent we have become, many of us have discarded those emblems that identify us with the larger society. This is the so-called age of individualism. The egocentric age of the "me" generation. All that matters is "me, myself and I." I can do what I want and it's nobody else's business. I have the right to be myself. If I want to smoke a crack pipe, it's none of your business—it's my body. If I want to move into my girlfriend's "crib," it's none of your business—we are both consenting adults. If I want to wear a micro-mini, it's none of your business—it's my prerogative. If I want to drive down the street playing gangsta beats and dance-hall vibes at 300 Watts on my car stereo, it's none of your business—its my car. If I want to fool around with that married man, it's none of your business—I'm the one taking the risk.

Unfortunately, this notion of individualism has so permeated our societies that many of us have forgotten the reality that "no man is an island." In our efforts to distance ourselves from conformity to society, we tend to forget that we are products of society. As much as you may feel like an individual, someone had to make those jeans that are five sizes too big for you. Someone had to make those shears that you used to fashion that funky fade. Someone had to manufacture the steel and refine the wood that are used to construct the instruments that play the new wave music you find so fascinating. No man is an island. Every one of us needs somebody.

In fact, it is out of this recognition of co-dependence that communities are born. Without communities, none of us could survive. Sociologists recognize that the most basic form of administrative communities is the village. Villages differ from towns or cities inasmuch as they are comprised of small groups of people who have lived together for generations. So fused are the lives of the villagers that in many areas they share the same values and goals.

If we were to visit the motherland, we would encounter village communities that have remained the same for centuries. After hundreds of years, the elders still gather by the gate to reason with each other and settle differences. Certain days are still set aside for sacrifices and festivities. Farmers still plow the fields with an ox and a wooden plough. God is still petitioned in times of famine and times of plenty.

Some of us who have been negatively influenced by Western modernism will frown at these people and scorn them for being backwards. But ask yourself these questions: "How many of these villagers are dying from strokes or hypertension?" "How many of them have been afflicted with cancer?" "How many of them are being harassed by debt collectors?" The truth is, these people have found a system that works for them—a system that has allowed them to maintain their traditions and values through countless generations. I believe that as long as these values remain, their village will remain. But if these values are ever overcome by the enchantment of industrialization and technology, that village will cease to exist.

The survival of the village is of extreme importance to the villagers, for in maintaining the village they are honoring the ancestors. In maintaining the village they are affirming the truth of the teachings and values that had been passed on to them. And so they realize that in order for the village to continue perpetually, the ones who are born into the village must share the village mentality. It is out of this desire that the birth of a child becomes a community event. It is generally accepted that children are not just born into nuclear families, but they are born into a community. Indeed, if the values of the community are to survive, the whole village must participate in the rearing and nurturing of the newborn infant. Hence, a famous proverb has arisen among several people groups in West Africa: "It takes an entire village to raise a child."[1]

Defining the Village

The village that concerns us today is the church of the living God. When we renounced the world and our sinful passions and were immersed in the watery grave of baptism, we gave up our citizenship in this world. We renounced our affiliation with all earthly potentates and entered into one of the communities that comprise the United States of Eternal Life. We entered into a global village encompassing numerous smaller village units inhabited by people who claim to love the Lord.

But what is the nature of this village? In spite of the atrocious confusion we often witness in the Church of God today, the village that we voluntarily joined is not an anarchy.

In spite of the fact that everyone wants to be the pastor, it is not a village in which each person can do what is right in his or her own eyes. It is a village that has a constitution. It is a village that has traditions and values. And the one who established this village is not the great African builder Nimrod, it is not the tyrannic Greek conqueror, Alexander the Great, it is not the megalomaniac German dictator, Hitler, but it is God himself. And in the tens and thousands of villages around the globe that see God as their founder, the Father of creation has mandated that the values and traditions that are central to the survivability of the village be passed on from generation to generation.

When we realize the importance of the survivability of the village, we have to come to terms with the fact that our children are the greatest resource that the village has. Children are not products of one-night stands who are to be left home alone while the parents go out partying. Children are not merely the physical expressions of two peoples' love for each other. Children are not objects to be seen and not heard. Children are not cute dolls for adults to adorn and admire. Children are not actors who are placed on the stage of life to make adults laugh with their mischievous antics. Children are gifts from God. By giving us children, God invites us into partnership with Him as we assist Him in helping them to find their place in His village.

Education of the Village Children

Naturally, the home in which the child was born will provide the primary context for the child's induction into the ways of the village. Every parent in God's village has a responsibility to shape the identity of the child entrusted to him or her. And even as they make choices for their children, parents need to know that "Barney" and "Sesame Street" cannot reveal to the child his true identity. "The Lion King" or "Sponge Bob" cannot assist the child in finding herself. Instead, from an early age, you should create an environment for your children to find an identity in the same God who spoke to Samuel (1 Sam 3:1-10). They should learn to seek the favor of the very God who empowered the little exiled servant girl to minister to Naaman (2 Kgs 5:1-5).

Rather than invest in the arduous challenges of parenting, many parents find it easier to pacify their children by placing them in front of a television set all day. The proliferation of so called "Christian" videos lends to the justification of this practice, as children are exposed to a biblical world that is void of Black people (and we wonder why so many join extreme Black cults or turn their backs on religion when they become inquiring teenagers). Christian entertainment has its place, but there is nothing that replaces the personal contact with our children as we take personal responsibility to transmit the stories of the ancestors to them.

While the home should be children's first school, children also need to be taught of the Lord when they go to the village school. The vision of God's ideal village in Isaiah is one in which "All the children are taught of the LORD" (54:13). Unfortunately, in this hedonistic and materialistic world in which we live, the philosophy is different. While the word of God says "All the children shall be taught of the LORD," the world states "All the children must be taught of the devil."

When we send our children to the schools of the world, they don't learn, "In the beginning God created," but "In the beginning a single cell amoeba multiplied." They don't learn about fleeing fornication, but are inducted in the ways of correct condom usage and "safe" sex. They don't learn about Adam and Eve and the sanctity of male-female marriage, but they read books like "My Two Mommies" and "My Daddy's New Roommate is Peter." They don't learn about the ethics of love, kindness, and sharing, but are taught to be power hungry capitalists who must win at every cost. They don't learn about the miracle of life beginning at conception, but are taught that abortion is a woman's choice. It is precisely because of the dichotomy between the philosophies of God's village and the secular global village that the Word of God makes us know that we cannot leave it up to society to fashion our children into citizens of the kingdom. If we intend to do our part in ensuring the survival of the village that God has entrusted to us, we will make sure that our children are taught of the LORD.

It is for this very reason that God has inspired forward thinking Christians to establish educational institutions for our children. These institutions provide a safe environment for those children who are making the transition from the secure environs of home to the uncertain playing field of society. While attending Church school, the impressionable minds won't be bombarded with negative peer pressure, but will be in an environment shared by people with like aspirations. Since Christian schools are an important factor in the transmission of the mores of the community, they should be accessible to all members of the village. The text does not say that only a privileged few shall be taught of the Lord, but "*all* of our children should be taught of Him." In other words, Christian education should not be a luxury for the sons and daughters of the wealthy, but it should be the right of every boy or girl who is associated with the village.

If we are really concerned about the eternal life of these young ones who did not even ask to be bought into the world, we will ensure that they receive a God-centered education. Sometimes we think that we can send them to a worldly school because of the school's reputation. But what about your child's character? The school may challenge them to be model citizens of the USA as they pledge allegiance to the flag, but would it encourage them to give their lives to Jesus? The contemporary secular school system is designed to promote a godless ethic. Furthermore, in many government schools, our children who are going through vulnerable and impressionable stages in their lives are forced to enter a war zone every day. Every day the ethical standards of their village are being challenged. Every day they are faced with the temptation of compromise and submission. And sadly, every day thousands of our young people give in to the peer pressure because they are fed up with being the odd one out. I submit that we serve our children better if we provide them with the opportunity to learn in an environment in which teachers and staff are concerned about their eternal destiny. Charting an academic path for your children through prestigious schools may eventually get them six figure salaries, but what will their wages be in the judgement?

Our Responsibility to the Village School

Before I continue, let me state that I am well aware that attendance at a Christian school does not guarantee your child a place in the kingdom. For many different reasons, the wheat and the tares co-exist among the student body, faculty, staff, and administration. No school provides that perfect environment. Some hormone possessed young man may still get a not-so-innocent young lady pregnant. Some inner city wannabee may bop around like a pseudo-gang banger. Some egomaniac seeking attention may experiment with cigarettes or alcohol. These things may happen, because people who do not share the ethos of the village are associated with the school. However, in spite of the obstacles, it is still a place where the students can testify about the goodness of God without being censored. It is still a place where classes are started with prayer. It is still a place where God is praised throughout the day.

The fact that our schools are not immune from the devil's ploys means that we are to hold our schools accountable. Since this is the village school, we all need to have an interest in its daily administration and mission. Our children should not be getting an inferior education, but should be able to stand head and shoulders above others who have been educated in public and other private schools. Our education should be an education with a difference. We should ensure that our schools have the best equipment and an accountable teaching staff so that our children will indeed be taught of the LORD. Our schools should have a niche that others cannot fill, and all of our children should have the opportunity to benefit.

I know there are some readers who may be intellectually persuaded by what I have said. They realize that Christian education is what their children deserve, but they feel they should get it for free. However, what they need to realize is that it costs to educate a child. Not only do the buildings need to be maintained and enhanced, but the teachers need to be paid. And believe me, many of us who work in Christian education are earning between 30 to 70% less than we could be earning elsewhere. However, we realize our responsibility to our village. We realize that our children are precious, because they are *our* children. We want to do our part in securing the stability of *our* village.

Conclusion

Since our faith communities comprise *our* village, any school associated with our church is *our* school. All who belong to a faith community must embrace the reality that we are our "brother's keeper." The implications of duty to our fellow humans is powerfully demonstrated in the account of the early church in Acts 2. Luke informs us that when the Holy Spirit fell on the saints, their entire concept of family was transformed. In a miraculous instant, they saw each other as brothers and sisters—members of the same village. It didn't matter to them that the members of the village originally hailed from Huntsville, Memphis, California, New York, Jamaica, Trinidad, Zimbabwe or India. Their place of origin was inconsequential. Their only concern was their shared destination. All that mattered to them was that they were united on the same path as they marched to Zion.

Fellow Christian, we claim to be marching to Zion today but I have news for you. Only those who have been baptized with the Holy Ghost can keep up with the pace. The true citizens of Zion recognize that they have a role to play in this temporary earthly village in which we live. This role involves ensuring that every young man and woman in our village has access to a Christian education. The time has come for village parents to make educational choices that will help and not harm their offspring. The time has come for those who may not have children to offer assistance to a family that has many. The time has come for those whose children have already graduated from school to assist another child through school. The time has come for those who have just graduated from college—and have landed their first well-paying job—to buy one less outfit or pair of shoes each month so that a child can receive an education. We do this, because we embrace our responsibility and know that if the village is to survive, the entire village must do its part in raising the village children.

STUDY QUESTIONS

1.   What is the central message of this chapter?

2.   How would your present faith community be different if it modeled itself after the early Christians' depicted in Acts 2:44-45?

3.   Is it possible to promote community responsibility in this age of the "nuclear family" when most church members only see each other once a week?

4.   While advancements in technology have definitely been a benefit to humanity, in what ways have they hurt the community? Is it fair to refer to non-industrialized nations with the term "underdeveloped"?

[The European myth suggests that true civilizations are those that are driven by technology. However, experience has shown that technology has devastated the community with its alienation of individuals and replacement of humans with machines. The successes of technology are easily overshadowed by the failures that are demonstrated by the increase in immorality, crime, pollution, human dependency, obesity, selfishness, etc.]

5.   Why is it essential for a member of the community to surrender his/her individual will to the constitution that governs that community?

6.   Discuss the five most important factors that should be considered *before* a couple decides to bring children into this world.

7.   What is your reaction to the suggestion that every village member is responsible for the nurture of the village children? Should the shared responsibility include disciplining children? How would you react if a concerned individual disciplined your child?

8.   What are the dangers faced by Christian children who attend public schools? What are the advantages of a Christian education?

9.   What can be done in your present faith community to ensure that every child has access to Christian education? (Consider 1 Timothy 5:8 in your answer.)

[Christian education is often prohibitive because the financial burden is left on the parents of children who attend the schools. If the expense were shared by the entire church, all of our children would be able to receive a godly education. In our stewardship, as we deny self of vain indulgences, we need to remember that "charity begins at home." The first "mission field" is your home territory.]

10.   In addition to contributing financially, what can you do to ensure that the village children get a quality Christian education?

11.   Reflect on how this chapter has affected you as a person.

12.   Evaluate how this chapter has affected your relationship with God.

CHAPTER EIGHT

THE WALLS CAME TUMBLING DOWN

*For he is our peace, in his flesh he has made both groups into
one and has broken down the dividing wall,
that is, the hostility between us.*
(Ephesians 2:14)

1993 was the closest I have ever come to experiencing the year of Jubilee. For the first time in the history of the fabricated nation that the English named "South Africa," democratic elections had taken place. History had been altered, and the majority had finally been given an opportunity to govern. For many, this was cause to celebrate as they saw an opportunity for a multi-cultural society of equal opportunity for all people. Many Coloreds and Blacks voted for F. W. DeKlerk as he campaigned as the "White Chief," and many Whites and Indians supported African National Congress Leader, Nelson Mandela.

This was not the first time in recent history that an event of such great proportion had occurred. Fifteen years after Ian Smith announced Rhodesia's Unilateral Declaration of Independence from the British Crown on November 11, 1965, Robert Mugabe and Joshua Nkomo led the Black majority to dominance as Cecil Rhode's bastion of oppression was replaced with the newly liberated Zimbabwe.

We need not look so far, for less than two decades before Zimbabwean independence, Dr. Martin Luther King, Jr. and the SCLC led the march to fight the apartheid system that was entrenched and legalized in American society. Energized by sister organizations like the Student Nonviolent Coordinating Committee, the National Urban League, The National Association for the Advancement of Colored People, and the Nation of Islam, the Civil Rights Movement also attracted the sympathy of White liberals who became partners in the fight to tear down the walls of American apartheid.

Barriers in Society

Although significant victories have been won in the effort to improve race relations, progress has been very slow in the institutions that have prematurely announced liberation. It is true that many opportunities have been forged for Blacks who now have better access to higher education. There have even been a marked increase in the number of Blacks who fill management and administrative level quotas in the private and government sectors. However, not much has changed. In Zimbabwe and South Africa, Whites still control a disproportionate amount of the wealth, and in that region which has been blessed with an abundance of precious minerals, the majority of the Black inhabitants are plagued with squalor and poverty.[1]

The same is true for the United States of America that has mastered the rhetoric of fairness and equality, but where at the same time forty percent of Black children live in impoverished conditions in contrast to eleven percent of White children. Some are under the illusion that injustice and inequity are worn-out bywords, but in reality a disproportionate number of Blacks live in run-down ghettoes and are given no incentive to get out, instead being pacified with welfare and food stamps. Those in denial can talk about a color-blind society, but no matter how much money a Black person makes or how famous he becomes, when it comes down to the crunch, he is still just a "nigger." Ask Mike Tyson, O. J. Simpson and Colin Powell if you don't believe me! It has become crystal clear that it doesn't matter how many theoretical walls are pulled down; it doesn't matter how many Civil Rights acts are passed and amended; it doesn't matter how many leaders envision a society free of racial prejudice, when we wake up the next morning—the next year—the next decade—the next century, we still come face to face with those towering invisible brick barriers that separate us from our fellow human beings.

Barriers in the Church

These evil cancers of segregation and false notions of superiority are no respecters of institutions, for they have even permeated those same religious systems that proclaim to be living out the gospel of Jesus Christ—I'm referring to our churches! In the very place that professes to be the body of a loving Lord, racism and separationist attitudes have reared their ugly heads.

Not many denominations have escaped this ecclesiastical racism. In 1793, Richard Allen and Absalom Jones were forcefully moved from a Methodist church when they tried to join the White people in prayer rather than stay in their assigned places in the balcony, and the African Methodist Episcopal Church came to birth. Three years later in the state of New York, James Varrick, upset by the racism of the Methodist church he held dear, broke away and established the African Methodist Episcopal Zion Church. The same happened with the Baptist Church leading to the formation of the National Baptist Convention (1886), and later the Church of God in Christ (1897). Further, as a result of the racist attitudes and practices of some of the European church leaders in the past, even the evangelistically minded Seventh-day Adventist Church was forced to officially segregate in 1945. More recently (1989), the Catholic church experienced fracture when Archbishop George Stallings, Jr. formed the Imani Temple in our nation's capital.[2]

As a result of ingrained racism, the majority of Christians in this nation have chosen to practice apartheid every week while attending church. All around the nation we are segregated into Black churches, White churches, Asian churches, Spanish churches, Native American churches, and the list goes on. Even among the various ethnic groups we find Polish churches, Caribbean churches, Korean churches, African-American churches and other sub-cultural fellowships. A person is hard pressed to locate a church community that is comprised of people from several ethnic backgrounds. Rather than showing the world how good and pleasant it is for brothers and sisters of all races to dwell together in unity, we are building little bushes under which we hide our lights. We claim to have the truth among other religions, but the truth obviously does not have us.

This fabrication of walls of hate and suspicion between churches of different races has led to the sad, but true, charge made by the historian, C. Eric Lincoln, who noticed that the Christian worship service is the most segregated hour in the life of America. We work together in the same offices or factories. We clean their homes and look after their children. We fix their cars and mow their lawns. We supervise their work and teach them in schools. We serve and protect them and perform delicate surgeries when they are afflicted with disease. But come church time, they go to their blanched cathedrals in the suburbs, and we to our humble chapels in urban America.

Unfortunately for many Blacks, the stigma of racism follows them into the pews of their places of worship. In too many congregations, our children are subjected to print resources that depict a biblical world predominated with Europeans. And in many of our sanctuaries, when we lift up our heads to praise the Lord, we are confronted with stain glass windows that depict a biblical world and heavenly universe fashioned after the country-club mentality of exclusion.

The sad thing is, we have become so conditioned to the psychological reminder that Europeans have redefined Christian culture that as soon as someone shows a picture of a Black Jesus—or any other biblical scene depicting Black people, we express our disgust by asking, "who really knows what color He was?"

We were very comfortable seeing Him as blond-haired and blue-eyed over the years and never complained once. We never complained that the European artists who painted the pictures for religious books were apparently allergic to certain of the darker colors on their pallet—which were reserved for the devil and his angels. And now that artists are painting Jesus with darker skin and thicker lips; now that a more accurate depiction is finally portrayed; now that we are finally moving closer to the truth about the ethnic backgrounds of biblical characters; now that we are given a chance to develop pride in knowing that people who were the same color as we were a part of the biblical world; we reject the images, we get uncomfortable, and we say, "Who really knows what color He was?" We forget that Jesus was a human just like we, and try to make Him into some sort of chameleon with the compromising absurdity: "He was all colors." Or we go into a state of embarrassed denial, as we ask the question, "What difference does it make?"

I contend that it makes all the difference, for until we reject the lies of subordination that have been fed to us; until we perceive ourselves as equals under heaven as our heavenly Father intended it; until we open our eyes and see the psychological damage being wrought in our children who will grow up to choose a Black Mohammed over a White Jesus, we will never be able to tear down those walls that separate us. Until we take seriously the words of 1 John 3:1 and see ourselves as sons and daughters of God, and not sons and daughters of the allegedly cursed Ham; until we see ourselves as princes and princesses instead of descendants of slaves, we will never be able to love our neighbor since we will never know how to love ourselves.

Barriers that Affect Self image

At this point, I want all of my readers to be aware that it is not my intention to promote Black superiority. I firmly believe that all people on this earth were created in the image of God. And although throughout the course of history race and culture have been used as separation markers, Paul reminds us that in Christ all the ethnic walls have been broken down. There is no difference between Jew, Greek, Bahamian, Ghanaian, Chinese, Trinidadian, Vincentian, African-American or any other ethnic group in the sight of God (Col 3:11).

It is not my intention to advocate Black superiority, but I do intend to encourage Black pride. Please understand that Black pride is not the counterpart to the professed "White pride" of those who shamefully hide their faces under bleached bed sheets while burning crosses on lawns. Unlike "White pride," Black pride is not about denigrating other races in order to elevate our own. Black pride is about holding our head high in spite of the fact that our ancestors were enslaved; in spite of the fact that disadvantaged conditions deprived our parents of a college education; in spite of the fact that many ignorant people view us as one step above the evolution of monkeys; in spite of the fact that we are still second-class citizens in this world. Black pride is about knowing that in spite of all these obstacles, Jesus Christ has bought us with a price—his own life. This is the same price he paid for Queen Elizabeth and George W. Bush. As a consequence of this generous act of redemption, we have every reason under the sun to be proud—not just because of *who* we are, but because of *whose* we are.

Demolishing the Barriers in the Church

I emphasize the need for us to be proud of our identity because until we see ourselves as equals with those who oppress us, we will never be able to tear down the walls that separate. The time has come for us to love ourselves and start doing the business of Jesus Christ. We hear much talk about Christian evangelism, but what message are we preaching? What kind of religion are we inviting people to join? As long as we propagate segregation and make no effort to change, we are being hypocritical to the very substance of the gospel. According to the Seer of Patmos, ours is a message that is intended to reach every "nation, ethnicity, tongue and people" (Rev 14:6-7). But what is the message that we preach? If we listen to some people, we will get the impression that Christianity is limited to church attendance, singing in the choir, baptism and partaking in communion.

While these things are important, they do not comprise the everlasting gospel. The everlasting gospel heralds the good news that although the devil may have temporary control of this world, it belongs to God. What Satan does not realize is that his lease expired a long time ago, and in the near future God is going to abolish all earthly governments and establish His own kingdom. The gospel informs us that when Jesus was resurrected, He gave Satan a notice of eviction and snatched away the keys to hell and the grave. Then He commissioned the disciples to inform the entire world that we are under new management. "This gospel of the kingdom," He said, "shall be proclaimed to the entire world as a testimony, and then shall the end come" (Mt 24:14).

Our sole task, saints, as agents for God is to pronounce that God's kingdom is soon to be ushered in—a kingdom of peace and security; a kingdom that is free from racial prejudice; a kingdom where all people are welcome in spite of how thick their lips, thin their noses or slanted their eyes. This is the message of the kingdom. However, every week when we refuse to witness to people who are not of the same ethnicity as we; every week when we deliberately turn our backs on each other, we are saying to the world that we do not believe in the transforming power of the gospel of Jesus Christ. We are saying that we don't believe that "He has made of many, one nation by his blood" (Acts 17:26).

Few can deny the problem of racism in the church. However, if we are waiting for ecclesiastical administrators to find a solution, it is probably not going to happen. Those churches that have tried to legislate integration are as segregated now as they were fifty years ago. We will only experience a difference when *individual* Christians come to terms with the gospel mandate for unity and begin to view *all* in the body of

Christ as brothers and sisters. The truth is, until our hearts have undergone true conversion we will never know how to accept and love one another.

We are now living in the dawn of the twenty-first century. It is true that segregation, suspicion and hatred still exist, but I believe that God is ready to do a new thing. I believe that God is ready to pour out His Holy Spirit on those people who are willing and ready to accept Him. I believe that God is going to raise up an army of spiritual warriors from "every nation, ethnicity, tongue and people." I believe the time is coming when God's people will walk together in unity. But the change must begin at the grassroots level. The Civil Rights Movement was a grassroots movement; ask Martin Luther King and Malcolm X. The ANC emerged from a grassroots movement; ask Nelson Mandela and Joshua Nkomo. Jamaican liberation from the imperial vice of the British empire was a grassroots movement; ask Sir Alexander Bustamante and the Right Excellent Paul Bogle.

Similarly, any change that is going to take place in the Church has to start from the grassroots. When Jesus came to bring change to the world, He did not go to the bishops, presidents or presiding elders, but He went to the people. Jesus realized that in order for change to be meaningful and permanent, each person has to make an individual decision to submit to God. The head of your denomination can't do it for you. He can't force you to worship with people of other races. We the people need to take the initiative and go forth, knowing that just because our congregations may be historically Black, they don't have to operate under a policy of exclusion.

The church needs to be conscious about building the family of God. But it's up to you to tear down those walls. It's up to you to take the initiative. It's up to you to invite your brothers and sisters who don't look like you or eat the same kind of food as you do into your homes. Some may ask, "Why is this our responsibility?" "Why should we congregate with people who worship differently than we do?" "Why should we fellowship with those who look at us strange when we get happy in church?" Peter asked the same question when he received the vision on the roof in Acts 10, but God made him know that whether a person is "red, or yellow, black or white, all are precious in His sight." And to prove it, we are told by Paul in Ephesians 2:14 that "Jesus is our peace for He has made all nations one and has broken down the dividing wall of hostility."

Conclusion

We must always remember that although it may seem as if tall walls separate us; although we may live and worship on different sides of town, the walls came tumbling down a long time ago. When Jesus' blood was shed on Calvary, every man, woman, boy and girl who ever was and ever will be was reconciled unto God and each other. And because the walls have been broken down, I can dream with Dr. Martin Luther King, whose famous words I have adapted to end this chapter:

I say to you today, my friends, that in spite of the difficulties and frustrations of the moment I still have a dream. It is a dream deeply rooted in the vision of Christ our Savior. I have a dream that one day the Christian Church will rise up and live out the true meaning of its creed: "There is neither Jew nor Greek, there is neither slave nor free, there is neither male nor female, for we are all one in Jesus Christ" (Gal 3:28). I have a dream that one day in the church that claims to represent God, the sons of former slaves and the sons of former slave owners will be able to sit down together at the table of fellowship. I have a dream that one day even those church institutions that remind us of a desert sweltering with the heat of injustice and oppression, will be transformed into oases of freedom and justice. I have a dream that my little children will one day be members of a church where they will not be judged by the color of their skin but by the content of their character.

I have a dream today.

I have a dream that one day the church which claims to preach a transforming gospel will allow the gospel to transform it and will become a haven where little Black boys and little Black girls will be able to join hands together with little White boys and little White girls, and walk together as sisters and brothers.

I have a dream today.

I have a dream that one day "every valley will be exalted, and every hill and mountain made low, the rough places shall be made plain, and the crooked places will be made straight, and the glory of the Lord shall be revealed, and all flesh shall see it together."

This is our hope. This is the faith with which I shall continue my ministry. With this faith, we will be able to hew out of the mountain of despair a stone of hope. With this faith, we will be able to transform the jangling discords of our Church into a beautiful symphony of brotherhood. With this faith, we will be able to work together, struggle together, go through the Time of Trouble together, stand up for freedom together, knowing that Jesus will return one day.

This will be the day when God's children will be able to sing with new meaning, "Blest be the tie that binds, our hearts in Christian love" And if the Church of God is to really represent His will in this present evil age, this vision of unity must become true. So, break down those walls in the ivory towers of the suburban cathedrals. Break down those walls in the bleached board rooms of the denominational administrators. Break down those walls in the fragile structures of the rural chapels. Break down those walls in the safe havens of the store-front churches. But not only that; break down those walls in the ebony structures of the urban worship centers. Break down those walls in every institution and member of this mighty movement. In every church and every parish, break down those walls.

When we break down those walls, when we break down those walls in all of our schools and hospitals, from every state and every city we will be able to speed up that day when all of God's children, Black men and White men, Jews and Gentiles, Protestants and Catholics shall come out of Babylon and its confusion, shall move out of darkness into light; shall move out of discord into the harmonious Church of the redeemed; and be able to join hands and sing in the words of the old Negro spiritual, "Free at last! Free at last! Thank God almighty, we are free at last!"

STUDY QUESTIONS

1.   What is the central message of this chapter?

2.   Carefully examine Ephesians 2:11-21 and Galatians 3:27-29. In light of these verses, can any ethnic group claim to be chosen by God?

[Joseph Smith, founder of the Mormons, claimed that White Americans are God's chosen people. A similar declaration was made by Herbert Armstrong, founder of the World Wide Church of God, who taught that people of Anglo-British descent have been favored by God. Many Ashkenazi (European) Jews also make this assertion. Among Black religions, we have the various Nations of Islam and the Hebrew Israelites professing divine privilege for Black people. However, according to the Bible, God has not chosen any "race" of people. Although technically comprised of Abraham's descendants, even ancient Israel was a multi-ethnic faith community that included people from many nationalities.]

3.   Define racism. Is it possible for Blacks to be racists in this society?

[Many people confuse racism with prejudice. Racism is only possible when one ethnic group has the political, economic, and military power to make the rules. Even those blacks who may espouse "racist" rhetoric are powerless. At the most, they are "potential racists."]

4.   What are the long-term effects of our children being exposed to religious material that portray all biblical characters as Western Europeans? Does the color of Christ really matter? Would our children be benefitted if *all* the biblical characters were painted Black?

5.   Do you agree with the author's suggestion that it is necessary for Christian Black people to have a healthy Black pride? Is it O.K. for White people to exhibit "White pride"?

[Black pride is very different from "White pride." White pride is the term used by White supremacists to promote the superiority of one race over another. Adversely, terms like "Black pride," and "Black power" are used to celebrate the endurance of Black people through their years of oppression.]

6. According to Revelation 14:6, how many ethnic groups have been given the invitation to be a part of God's family? Can we really call ourselves Christians if we continue to practice apartheid in our church communities?

7. According to John 13:34-35, what is the *true* sign of Christ's disciples?

[Some Christian groups say that the sign of true Christianity is tongue speaking, Sabbath-keeping, or some other external manifestation. However, Jesus says that the only genuine sign of Christianity is a community that is governed by love.]

8. Discuss five things *you* can do to foster racial reconciliation among members of the Church of God.

9. Reflect on how this chapter has affected you as a person.

10. Evaluate how this chapter has affected your relationship with God.

ENDNOTES

We've Come This Far by Faith

1.M. Scott Peck, *The Road Less Traveled: A new psychology of love, traditional values, and spiritual growth* (New York: Simon & Schuster, 1978).

2.L. Ron Hubbard, *Dianetics, the Modern Science of Mental Health: a handbook of Dianetics procedure*, 2nd ed. (Los Angeles: Bridge Publications, 1985).

3.For the full context of this statement and a balanced commentary, see James W. Loewen, *Lies My Teacher Told Me* (New York: Simon & Schuster, 1995), 180-85.

4.See James M. Cone, *Martin & Malcolm & America: A Dream or a Nightmare* (Maryknoll, NY: Orbis, 1991).

5.On love as a strategy for fighting evil systems, see Keith Burton, *The Compassion of the Christ* (Grantham: Stanborough Press, 2004), 87-90.

6.See Cone, *Martin & Malcolm & America*.

It's Time

1.See Charles Bradford, *Sabbath Roots: The African Connection* (Washington, DC: GC Ministerial Department, 1999).

2.Na'im Akbar, *Breaking the Chains of Psychological Slavery* (Tallahassee, FL: Mind Productions & Associates, 1996).

3.Owusu-Mensa, Kofi. *Saturday God and Adventism in Ghana* (Frankfurt/New York: Peter Lang, 1993).

An Affirmation of Black Manhood
1.See James H. Jones, *Bad Blood: The Tuskegee Syphilis Experiment* (New York: Simon & Schuster, 1993).

2.See Boyd E. Graves, *State Origin: The Evidence for the Laboratory Birth of AIDS* (Abilene, KS: Zygote Media Networks, 2001).

Hakuna Matata
1."The Lion King" was directed by Roger Allers and Rob Minkoff, with a screenplay by Irene Mecchi, Jonathan Roberts and Linda Woolverton, and produced by Don Hahn. It was released by Walt Disney Pictures.

2.Richard J. Herrnstein and Charles Murray, *The Bell Curve: Intelligence and Class Structure in American Life* (New York: The Free Press, 1994).

3.See the first volume of her autobiography in *I Know Why the Caged Bird Sings* (New York: Bantam Books, 1971).

4.See Noble Alexander and Kay D. Rizzo, *I Will Die Free* (Omaha: Pacific Press Publishing Association, 1991).

5.Ellen G. White, *Education* (Mountain View, CA: Pacific Press Publishing Association, 1903), 57.

Worldly Wine for a Perishing People
1.Words by James Weldon Johnson (1871-1938) and music by J. Rosamond Johnson (1873-1954). For full text, see J. Jefferson Cleveland and Verolga Nix, eds. *Songs of Zion* (Nashville: Abingdon Press, 1981).

2.Curtis Burrell, "I Don't Feel No Ways Tired," in Cleveland and Nix, *Songs of Zion*.

3.Ellen G. White, *Life Sketches of Ellen G. White* (Mountain View, CA: Pacific Press Publishing Association, 1902), 196.

4.For instance, see Dee Miles, "Bill Cosby attacks poor African Americans," *People's Weekly World Newspaper Online* (June 26, 2004), http://www.pww.org/ article/ view/ 5425/ 1/ 221/, who writes, "...Cosby's behavior in issuing such an account is as bad as that of the worst misguided Black youth whose stereotyped and caricatured behavior he universalizes."

5.Margaret Pleasant Douroux, "What Shall I Render," in Cleveland and Nix, *Songs of Zion*.

6.Clara Ward, "How I Got Over," in Cleveland and Nix, *Songs of Zion*.

We Shall Overcome
1.See Cheikh Anta Diop, *The African Origin of Civilization: Myth or Reality*, trans. Mercer Cook (New York: Hill, 1974).

2.Bradford, *Sabbath Roots*.

One Village, One Child
1.Hilary Rodham Clinton, *It Takes a Village: And Other Lessons Children Teach Us* (New York: Simon & Schuster, 1996), capitalized on this African proverb. Interestingly, her husband, President William Jefferson Clinton, also benefitted from African resources when he received a Rhodes Scholarship to Oxford. The Rhodes Scholarship is named after Cecil Rhodes, the infamous exploiter of African gold and diamonds.

The Walls Came Tumbling Down
1.For an interesting commentary see Thami Ka Plaatjie, "Conference to Build the ASI - Report from Azania (South Africa)," *The Burning Spear Newspaper*, http://burningspear-uhuru.com/0603_azania.htm.

2.For a concise introduction to the history of African American denominations, see articles in Larry Murphy, J. Gordon Melton, and Gary Ward, eds., *The Encyclopedia of African-American Religions* (Garland Publishing Company, 1993).

GLOSSARY

Affirmative Action. A civil rights law that guarantees jobs and access to public services for minorities.

African Methodist Episcopal Church. Black Methodist church founded by Richard Allen in 1794.

African Methodist Episcopal Zion Church. Black Methodist church founded in 1796 by James Varrick, Peter Williams, George Collins and Christopher Rush.

African National Congress (ANC). African liberation group instrumental in securing independence for colonized Southern African states.

Allah. The Arabic word for God. The preferred name for God by Black Moslems.

Allen, Richard. Founder of the African Methodist Episcopal Church.

Angelou, Maya. Black author, poet, and educator.

Apartheid. The doctrine that ethnic groups in the same country should live and work separately. *See* **Segregation.**

Augustine of Hippo. A North African theologian of the early Christian church.

Azania. Another name for South Africa.

Bell Curve. A controversial book that questions the intelligence of Black people.

Bennet, Lerome. Popular Black historian and editor of *Ebony Magazine.*

Black History Month. Persuaded by the efforts of Carter G. Woodson, Congress approved the month of February for the celebration of Black history.

Bogle, Paul. Jamaican national hero who led the Morant Bay Rebellion against British oppression in 1865.

Bradford, C. E. The first Black to serve as president for the North American Division of Seventh-day Adventists.

Brown vs. Board of Education. A historic decision that established the precedent for integration in all American public institutions.

Bustamante, Alexander. Jamaican trade unionist, civil rights activist, and Prime Minister.

Carver, George Washington. African-American scientist who developed countless uses for the peanut.

Castro, Fidel. Communist leader of Cuba.

Civil Rights Act. Act passed by Congress in 1964 guaranteeing equal rights for all citizens of the United States of America.

Civil Rights Movement. Term given to the Black struggle for equality in the United States of America and that took place in the 1950s-60s.

Cleveland, E. E. Accomplished author and evangelist of the Seventh-day Adventist Church.

Cochrane, Johnny. Black attorney who successfully defended O. J. Simpson from charges that he killed his wife, Nicole, and her friend, Ronald Goldman, in a much publicized 1995-96 trial.

Cone, James. Black theologian who teaches at Columbia University, New York. Author of *Black Theology and Black Power*.

Connors, Bull. Racist sheriff from Birmingham, Alabama, who ordered the violent attack of Civil Rights activists as they peacefully protested.

Cudjoe. A Jamaican freedom fighter of the eighteenth century who successfully revolted against the British. See *Nanny*.

Curse of Ham. The erroneous myth that Black people have been cursed by God through Noah.

Dancehall Music. A type of Jamaican reggae that promotes violence and immorality.

DeKlerk, F. W. A former president of South Africa under whose regime Apartheid ceased.

Dorsey, Thomas. Celebrated gospel music composer who penned the moving song "Precious Lord."

Douglass, Frederick. Black abolitionist, autobiographer, and editor who was elected president of the New England Anti-Slavery Society in 1847.

Dubois, William E. B. Black activist and intellectual. Founder of the Niagra Movement (forerunner to the NAACP). Renowned author of *Souls of Black Folk*. See *Talented Tenth*.

Egyptian Coptic Church. State church of Egypt.

Emancipation Proclamation. A proclamation granting freedom for slaves. Granted in the British empire in 1833 and in the United States of America in 1863.

Ethiopian Orthodox Church. State church of Ethiopia. Possibly the oldest state church in Christendom.

Evers, Medgar. Leader of the Mississippi NAACP who was assassinated in 1963.

Fahd, Wallace. Founder of the Nation of Islam in 1929.

Farrakhan, Louis. Third national leader of the major denomination of the Nation of Islam.

Father Divine. Black cult leader who founded the Peace Mission Movement in 1919.

Felder, Cain Hope. Prominent Black theologian who teaches at Howard University. Author of *Troubling Biblical Waters*, and editor of *The Original African Heritage Bible*.

Forty acres and a mule. Reparations promised to the newly emancipated Blacks by the United States government.

Foy, William. A Black Baptist pastor and follower of William Miller who received visions of the second coming of Christ in the 1840s.

Fuhrman, Mark. Racist police officer who strongly affected the outcome of the O. J. Simpson murder trial.

Gangsta Rap. An African-American art form that glorifies violence.

Garvey, Marcus. Pan-African political activist and founder of the Universal Negro Improvement Association in the early to mid-1900s.

Gottwald, Norman. European theologian who claims that the stories in the Bible are myth and not history.

Gutiérrez, Gustavo. Latin American liberation theologian who claims that God favors the cause of oppressed people.

Harlem Renaissance. A black intellectual and cultural movement that started in the 1920s in Harlem, New York and lasted several decades.

Hush Harbor. The name given to the place where slaves would gather for worship.

Imani Temple. An independent Black Roman Catholic church.

Integration. The attempt to incorporate ethnic groups into American public life.

Islam. Seventh century religion founded by Mohammed in Saudi Arabia.

Jackson, Jesse. African-American civil rights activist, leader of the Rainbow Coalition, and former Shadow Senator for Washington, D.C.

Jackson, Mahalia. World renowned gospel singer.

Jefferson, George. Character played by Sherman Hemsley in a 1970s sitcom.

Johnson, James Weldon. Co-author with his brother Rosamond of Negro national anthem, "Lift Every Voice and Sing."

Jones, Absalom. Episcopalian priest and associate of Richard

Allen, founder of the African Methodist Episcopal Church.

Jones, Jim. Church of the Nazarene pastor and cult leader who led mass suicide in Guyana, South America.

Kalinjeni. A Kenyan tribe with a history of Sabbath-keeping.

King, Jr., Martin Luther. Undisputed leader of the American Civil Rights Movement.

Kisekka, Samson. Ugandan revolutionist, Prime Minister, and Seventh-day Adventist physician.

Koran. The major Moslem holy book.

Ku Klux Klan. A white supremacist group.

L'Ouverture, Toussaint. Liberationist of the eighteenth century who led Haiti's revolution against France.

Lemba. A tribe in southern Africa that claims Israelite ancestry.

Lincoln, Abraham. United States president who endorsed the emancipation of slaves in 1863.

Lincoln, C. Eric. Authoritative Black historian.

Mandela, Nelson. Exiled leader of the ANC who became the first democratically elected president of the People's Republic of South Africa in 1993.

Marley, Robert Nesta "Bob". Jamaican musician and civil rights activist.

McCay, Claude. Jamaican poet of the Harlem Renaissance.

Muhammad, Elijah. First official minister of the nation of Islam.

Möltmann, Jurgen. Catholic liberation theologian.

Mugabe, Robert. Zimbabwean freedom fighter and nation's first co-leader.

Nanny of the Maroons. Jamaican freedom fighter of the eighteenth century.

Nation of Islam. Name of several groups that trace their origin to Wallace Fahd and Elijah Mohammed.

National Association for the Advancement of Colored People (NAACP). Civil rights group founded by William B. G. Dubois.

National Baptist Convention. Association of Black Baptists.

Negritude. Term coined by Marcus Garvey for "Black pride."

Negro Spirituals. Spiritual songs that fortified the hope of slaves in the United States of America.

Nkomo, Joshua. Zimbabwean freedom fighter and nation's first co-leader.

Nkrumah, Kwame. Leader of the Convention Party who spearheaded Ghanaian independence from the British.

Pan African Congress (PAC). African liberation party.

Parks, Rosa. "Mother" of the Civil Rights Movement whose refusal to sit at the back of a public bus in the segregated South sparked the Montgomery Bus Boycott.

Plessy vs. Ferguson. Landmark 1896 decision by the Supreme Court that enforced "separate but equal" policy and established American segregation.

Racism. The belief that the possession of economic, political, and military power is an indication that a certain ethnic group is superior to others.

Reconstruction. The rebuilding period after the Civil War when Blacks were briefly allowed the privileges of full citizenship.

Reverend Ike. Popular Black cult preacher in the 1970s, founder and pastor of the Christ United Church in New York.

Rhodesia. The name for Zimbabwe under British rule. Named for Cecil Rhodes, exploiter of southern Africa's resources.

Sabbath. The seventh day of the week.

Segregation. The practice of separating Blacks and Whites in the United States of America.

Selassie, Haile. Late emperor of Ethiopia, and founder of the Organization of African Unity in 1963.

Social justice. The belief that the poor and disenfranchised in a community should be given a voice.

Southern Christian Leadership Conference (SCLC). A Civil Rights group.

Talented Tenth. William DuBois' philosophy that promoted the intellectual development of ten percent of all Black people for the benefit of the entire group.

Thomas, Clarence. Second Black supreme court justice appointed in 1991 amidst controversy that he sexually harassed Anita Hill.

Truth, Sojourner. Champion of civil rights in the 1800s.

Tubman, Harriet. Celebrated leader of the underground railroad who helped many slaves to escape to freedom in the North.

Turner, Nat. Leader of 1831 slave rebellion.

Universal Negro Improvement Association (UNIA). Organization founded by Marcus Garvey in 1914 to improve the economic and political power of Africans around the globe.

Varrick, James. Co-founder of the African Methodist Episcopal Zion Church.

Venda. Ancient Zimbabwean kingdom.

Walker, David. African-American liberationist of the 1800s.

Washington, Booker T. Black educator and founder of Tuskegee University.

Weems, Renita. Black theologian. A specialist in Hebrew Bible at

Vanderbilt University.

X, Malcolm (El-Hajj Malik el-Shabbazz). Civil rights leader, minister in the Nation of Islam, founder of the American chapter of the Organization of African Unity.

INDICES

SCRIPTURE INDEX

117

GENERAL INDEX

Order Information

If your bookstore does not have *The Faith Factor*, you may order additional copies online at the *life*HERITAGE Store (www.lifeheritage.org/store), or you can send your prepaid order to:

> *life*HERITAGE Ministries
> P.O. Box 56
> Harvest, AL 35749

Copies	Price	Postage*
1-5	10.99	10%
6-10	9.99	5%
11-20	9.99	Free
21-30	8.99	Free
31-50	7.99	Free

Special rates are available for church and community group fundraisers. All requests must be made on the official letterhead of the sponsoring organization, and must be for a minimum of 100 books. Requests may be mailed to the address above, or sent as an e-mail attachment to faithfactor@lifeheritage.org.

*Postage rates do not apply to international orders.

Author Information

Dr. Keith Augustus Burton is available for preaching, seminars, motivational speaking, workshops, lectures, and interviews. You may contact him by mail at the address above, or by sending an e-mail to speaker@lifeheritage.org. Direct reservations can be made at www.lifeheritage.org.